M782.27 Shape Wyeth.J

Wyeth, John, 1770-1858.

Repository of sacred music, part second. 1964.

DEC 1 2 1980

EVANSTON PUBLIC LIBRARY

EVANSTON, ILLINOIS

Two cents a day is charged for adult books kept over time; one cent a day for children.

The borrower is responsible for books charged to his name and for mutilation unless reported at time of issue.

WYETH'S
REPOSITORY OF SACRED MUSIC
PART SECOND

Jno Wyeth

WYETH'S
REPOSITORY OF SACRED MUSIC

PART SECOND

With a New Introduction to the Da Capo Edition by

IRVING LOWENS
Music Division
Library of Congress

EVANSTON PUBLIC LIBRARY
1703 ORRINGTON AVENUE
EVANSTON, ILLINOIS

Da Capo Press
NEW YORK
1964

A Da Capo Reprint Edition

An unabridged republication of the Second Edition (1820) originally published by John Wyeth at Harrisburg, Pennsylvania.

This edition has been made from an original copy in the Irving Lowens Musical Americana Collection of The Moravian Music Foundation, Inc., Winston-Salem, North Carolina, and is reproduced by courtesy of The Foundation.

Library of Congress Catalog Card Number 64-18989

*©1964 Da Capo Press
A Division of Consultants Bureau Enterprises, Inc.
227 West 17th Street
New York, N.Y. 10011*

Printed in the United States of America

*For V.E.L.,
who knows why.*

INTRODUCTION

The American folk-hymn (or spiritual folk-song, as it was christened by the late George Pullen Jackson) is basically a secular folk-tune which happens to be sung to a religious text. In many cases the text is also folk derived, but not infrequently it is drawn from the body of orthodox hymns found in the hymnals of earlier days. The music, however, is almost invariably of folk origin, and its antecedents can be generally traced to the family of Anglo-Celtic folk-music, either vocal or instrumental.

The practice of singing religious texts to secular folk-tunes is more closely linked with the early history of American music than is usually realized. As early as the 1730's, folk-hymnody appears to have flourished, prospering under the impetus of the "Great Awakening," when Jonathan Edwards, George Whitefield, and other inflammatory preachers seared the religious conscience of New England. It is highly probable that folk-hymnody was an omnipresent phenomenon during the second half of the 18th century, although it is difficult to cite concrete written evidence to that effect. Certainly, the fact that the *composed* singing-school music of early America (beginning in the 1770's and mushrooming at a tremendous rate in the next three decades) was stylistically so closely akin to the folk-music of the British Isles, and hence to the folk-hymn, strongly suggests that such was the actual state of affairs. Furthermore, it is reasonable to assume that the highly characteristic style of composition practiced by Daniel Read, the Lewis Edsons, Jacob French, Oliver Brownson, Timothy Swan, Justin Morgan, and many others active in Connecticut and central Massachusetts during the 1780's and 1790's was based on the music they heard around them; the semi-folk idiom they cultivated was in all likelihood based on the music ingrained in their consciousness—Anglo-Celtic folk-music and its religious offshoot, American folk-hymnody.

Despite their popularity and widespread diffusion among the populace as a whole during the 18th century, folk-hymns do not seem to have achieved the permanence of print much before the beginning of the 19th. Folk-texts alone, as well as secular folk-tunes, had been published, but the peculiar combination of sacred text and lay tune only on very rare occasions.[1] It was not until after the second great wave of religious revivals swept the country around 1800 that the history of folk-hymnody in print actually began. The first compendia of folk-hymns were Northern collections, but very soon afterwards such collections began to appear in the South and the West of the time—Virginia, Tennessee, Kentucky, the Missouri Territory, Ohio, the Western Reserve. The transit of folk-hymnody from the North to the South seems to have taken place during the second decade of the 19th century, roughly coinciding with the retreat of the quasi-folk com-

---

[1] A few authentic folk hymns can be found in the tune-books of the late 1790's. See, for example, Amos Pilsbury's *The United States' Sacred Harmony* (Boston, 1799), which contains among others the first known printing of "Kedron," one of the loveliest and most popular of all folk-hymns. It is interesting to note that Pilsbury himself was a Southerner active in Charleston, South Carolina.

posed American music of the singing-schools from urban to rural surroundings. During the crucial decade, these two related types of music joined hands, so to speak, and ever since then the Yankee fuging-tune and psalm-tune are found side by side with the folk-hymn. In this form (later to be known *in toto* as the Southern folk-hymnody tradition) they became a prominent feature of Southern musico-religious life throughout the 19th century. Even today, the tradition is not yet extinct, although it must be said that it appears to be moribund.

The Southern history of the printed folk-hymn begins in 1815 or 1816 with the publication of Ananias Davisson's *Kentucky Harmony* at Harrisonburg, Virginia. Like contemporary Northern tune-books, it was brought out in the typical oblong format and contained a selection of various tunes and the customary introduction to the grounds and rules of music. The *Kentucky Harmony* was peculiarly distinctive in that its contents included a large number of authentic folk-hymns. It was an extremely popular book in the South; edition followed edition, and it left its mark on Southern folk-hymnody for decades to come. The extent of its influence can be gauged from George Pullen Jackson's classic study, *White Spirituals in the Southern Uplands* (Chapel Hill, N.C., 1933), which devotes many pages to tracing borrowings from its pages by later Southern compilers such as Carden, Boyd, Funk, Carrell, Moore, Walker, White, and King. The collections assembled by these men, as well as their individual teaching efforts and enthusiasm for the music they disseminated, were to a large degree responsible for the growth of the singing tradition throughout the South.

It can therefore be seen that an inquiry into the antecedents of these Southern tune-books (and of Davisson's *Kentucky Harmony* as the first of the Southern species, in particular) is of some genuine consequence despite the obscurity of the names of their compilers. As has been strongly hinted, the idea of printing folk-hymns was not original with Davisson; several men had preceded him in that field. Although Jeremiah Ingalls of New Hampshire has been generally credited with being the first to issue a collection which includes folk-hymns, primacy probably belongs to Samuel Holyoke, a more prominent New England compiler and singing-master. One of the lesser known of his half-dozen tune-books, *The Christian Harmonist* (Salem, Mass., 1804), which was specifically designed for the use of Baptist churches, contains a large number of folk-texts mostly selected from Joshua Smith's *Divine Hymns, or Spiritual Songs* (Norwich, N. H., 1784) set to a variety of folk-like tunes, many of which had never been previously printed. From a study of the content of the tune-book, it would appear that Holyoke here attempted to compose in the folk idiom, and it is quite possible that some of the tunes were notated directly from the oral tradition. The collection was not widely used, however, and it does not seem to have been known outside of northeastern Massachusetts and southeastern Vermont and New Hampshire. A similar fate greeted Ingalls' *Christian Harmony* (Exeter, N. H., 1805), which in all probability did not circulate much beyond the small orbit of the compiler's personal activity. There is some possibility that Ingalls was familiar with the Holyoke work, as he utilized many of the same texts, a few of the same tune-names, and perhaps modelled the title of his book after Holyoke's.

Neither of these tune-books, however, appears to have been known to Davisson at the time he compiled the *Kentucky Harmony*. Despite a similarity in character, there is virtually no duplication of musical content, and both Northern books must be eliminated as significant precursors of the *Kentucky Harmony*.

The progenitor of the Davisson collection is a third Northern tune-book, very little known even among specialists in early American music history, John Wyeth's *Repository of Sacred Music, Part Second* (Harrisburg, Pa., 1813;

INTRODUCTION

2nd edition, 1820, differing from the 1st only in minor details), which was published at least two (and possibly three) years before the *Kentucky Harmony* came from the presses. According to Wyeth, some 25,000 copies were eventually sold, a quite respectable figure in view of the fact that the population of Harrisburg in 1820 was only a little over 3,000. As the town was directly on the main line of emigration to the South and West, most of the copies of *Part Second* appear to have travelled in that direction rather than towards New England.

By 1813, when *Part Second* appeared, Wyeth was already known as a tune-book compiler because of several collections, the most popular of which was his *Repository of Sacred Music* (Harrisburg, Pa., 1810; six subsequent editions, the last of which appeared as late as 1834). The *Repository* was quite different in character from *Part Second* despite the similar name. One of the best-selling tune-books of the entire decade, it was primarily an eclectic collection of the best-liked American psalm- and fuging-tunes of the day, quite similar in character and content to many others of earlier years. Its immediate prototype seems to have been the famous *Easy Instructor*[2] "by" William Little and William Smith. From this tune-book, Wyeth borrowed the characteristic shape-note method of notation which was eventually to become standard in the South, where it was almost universally adopted. No new tunes are to be found in the pages of the *Repository*.

Superficially, there appears to be little difference between the *Repository of Sacred Music* and the *Repository of Sacred Music, Part Second*; the formats of the two are identical, and both make use of the Little and Smith shape-notes. In content, however, they are completely dissimilar. *Part Second* was something new in the tune-book field, an attempt to supply the musical needs of the vast market created by the revivals and camp-meetings so prevalent in Pennsylvania at the time. As such, it was a thoroughly distinctive collection, quite independent of the first *Repository*. Wyeth may have deliberately cultivated the confusion which arose between the two (*Part Second* is frequently mistaken, even today, for a second edition of the less important *Repository*) in an attempt to cash in on the popularity of the first *Repository*. That he was certainly aware of it is evident from the preface to *Part Second*, where he writes that "while introducing this second part, he by no means wishes it to be understood that the first is to be laid aside." *Part Second* might well be better known today had Wyeth given it a title as distinctive as its content.

An initial clue to the close relationship between Davisson's *Kentucky Harmony* and Wyeth's *Repository of Sacred Music, Part Second* can be found in the preface to the Southern collection. There Davisson lists the names of compilers with whose works he was familiar: Little, Smith, Wyeth, Billings, Holyoke,[3] Atwell,[4] and Peck,[5] in the order named. To these should be added (from an analysis of the content of the *Kentucky Harmony*) Daniel Read and Nehemiah Shumway.[6] Except for Wyeth's *Part Second*, none of the many tune-books compiled by the men cited contains any appreciable number of folk-hymns, and a comparative analysis of the Davisson and Wyeth books conclusively demonstrates that *Part Second* was

---

[2] For the full story of this most influential collection, see Irving Lowens and Allen P. Britton, "The *Easy Instructor* (1798-1831): A History and Bibliography of the First Shape-Note Tune-Book," *Journal of Research in Music Education*, I, 1 (Spring 1953), 30-55.

[3] As has been previously stated, the Holyoke collection with which Davisson was familiar was probably not *The Christian Harmonist*.

[4] Probably Thomas H. Atwill, compiler of *The New York and Vermont Collection*. A Richard Atwell is known as a composer, but no tune-book of his compilation has been discovered.

[5] Daniel L. Peck, compiler of *The Musical Medley* (Dedham, Mass., 1808) and *A Valuable Selection of Sacred Music* (Philadelphia, 1810).

[6] Compiler of *The American Harmony* (Philadelphia, 1793).

Table I
Key

- *WR2*   John Wyeth, *Repository of Sacred Music, Part Second* (1813)
- *DKH*   Ananias Davisson, *Kentucky Harmony* (ca. 1815)
- *BVR*   James M. Boyd, *The Virginia Sacred Musical Repository* (1818)
- *CMH*   Allen D. Carden, *The Missouri Harmony* (1820)
- *FGM*   Joseph Funk, *Genuine Church Music* (1832)
- *WSH*   William Walker, *The Southern Harmony* (1835)
- *WKH*   B. F. White and E. J. King, *The Sacred Harp* (1844)

Tune Name	WR2	DKH	BVR	CMH	FGM	WSH	WKH
*Adoration	?	Davisson[a]		X[a]			
*Animation	?						
Babylonian Captivity	Dare	Dare		X		Dare	
Band of Love[b]	?				X		
Bellevue	Dare			X			
Bridgetown	Dare						
*Christmas Hymn	?						
*Communion	Robison[c]				X[d]		X[d]
*Concert	?						
*Consolation (I)	?	Dean	X	X	X	Dean	Dean
*Consolation (II)	?					?	?[e]
*Davis	?			X		?	
*Dependence	Findlay						
*Dismission	Dare						
*Fairton	Dare						
Fall of Babylon	?						
Fidelia	Lewer			X			
*Fiducia	Robinson	Robertson	X		X	Robison	
*Forster	?		X	X			
*Glasgow	Dare	Davisson	X	X		Dare	
Gospel Trump	Dare						
*Hallelujah	?			X			
*Happiness	?						
*Heavenly Union	?						
*Kedron[f]	Dare	Davisson[g]	X			Dare	Dare
*Landaff	Findlay		X				
Liberty[h]	?	Wyeth		X		?	?
Marcus Hook	Dare						
*Messiah	?						
*Middle Paxton	Austin						

Note: First editions of these rather scarce tune-books were not available for purposes of comparison. Three of the above (*BVR*, *CMH*, and *FGM*) contain no composer attributions. Presence of an identical tune in any of these is indicated with an "X." Asterisked tunes are folk-hymns.

Tune Name	WR2	DKH	BVR	CMH	FGM	WSH	WKH
*Millville	Dare						
*Minister's Farewell[1]	?					?	?
*Morality[j]	?		X	X		?	?
Mount Hope	Dare						
*New Canaan	?	Davisson[k]		X[k]			
*New Monmouth	?	Billings		X	X		
Ninety-Fifth	Chapin	Chapin		X		Colton Chapin	Colton Chapin
*Ninety-Third	Chapin	Chapin		X		Chapin	Chapin
*Perseverance	?						
*Power	White						
Providence[l]	C. Curtis						
*Redeeming Grace	?				?		
Redemption Anthem	?	Stephenson[m]				A. Benham, Sr.	
*Restoration	?						
*Roadstown	Dare						
*Rockbridge	Chapin	Chapin		X	X	Chapin	
*Rockingham	Chapin	Chapin		X	X	Chapin[n]	
*Solicitude	?						
*Solitude	M'Kyes[o]		X				
*Spring Hill	?				X	?[d]	
*Sterling	?		X				
*Sublimity	?					?	
*Transport	?		X				
Triumph	?						
*Twenty-fourth	Chapin	Chapin[p]	X	X	X	Chapin[p]	Chapin[p]
*Unitia	Chapin		X	X			
*Vernon	Chapin		X	X	X	Chapin	Chapin
*Willington[q]	?						
Wilmington	Dare						

Notes
a) Called "Condescension."
b) Previously published, called "Washington," in Andrew Law's *Select Harmony* (Philadelphia, ca. 1811).
c) In the second edition the composer's name is given as "Robinson."
d) Variant.
e) Called "Consolation (New)."
f) Previously published in Amos Pilsbury's *The United States' Sacred Harmony* (Boston, 1799).
g) Variant, called "Garland."
h) Previously published in Stephen Jenks's *The Musical Harmonist* (New Haven, 1800).
i) Appears only in the 1st edition of *WR2*.
j) Previously published (with secular text) in A. Aimwell's (A. Adgate's) *The Philadelphia Songster* (Philadelphia, 1789), and frequently elsewhere, including England and Scotland, under the title "Alknomook," or "The Indian Chief." A very popular tune at the beginning of the 19th century, well known as "the death song of the Cherokee Indians."
k) Called "Reflection."
l) Not in *WR2* index; apparently substituted in the 2nd edition for "Minister's Farewell."
m) Truncated version.
n) *WKH* also includes a variant version, with the same name, claimed by Lowell Mason.
o) A misprint in the *WR2* index. Should read "M. Kyes."
p) Called "Primrose."
q) Previously published in James Lyon's *Urania* (Philadelphia, 1761) and elsewhere.

the salient folk-hymnodic influence in the content of the *Kentucky Harmony*.

Wyeth claims that 58 of the 149 tunes included in *Part Second*, more than one-third of the total number, are there published for the first time. The correctness of this assertion is of vital importance, because if it could be demonstrated that many of these were in actuality taken from earlier printed sources, the special role played by *Part Second* in the establishment of Southern folk-hymnody might be legitimately questioned. After a long search, however, I have been able to discover prior publication of only five[7] of these 58 tunes called "new" —certainly not a sufficient number to invalidate the general accuracy of the claim. When it is realized that no less than 44 of these 58 new tunes are quite definitely folk-hymns, *Part Second* begins to assume considerable significance.

Because this particular body of 44 folk-hymns began its printed existence on the pages of *Part Second*, the establishment of relationships between the Wyeth book and other later collections is a comparatively simple and clear-cut task. Table I shows the extent of the eventual dissemination of the folk-hymns first published by Wyeth (which include some of the finest and best known in the entire tradition) through a comparison of the new music in *Part Second* with the content of six important and representative later Southern tune-books.

[7] For identifications, see the notes to Table I.

A relationship between *Part Second* and the *Kentucky Harmony* is immediately evident. Davisson borrowed 15 tunes from Wyeth and, curiously enough, three of these are claimed as his own compositions. Two of these three tunes, "Adoration" and "New Canaan," are disguised under new names as "Condescension" and "Reflection"; the third, Dare's "Glasgow," appears with the same tune-name but is reprinted in a different key. The similarity in title between James M. Boyd's *The Virginia Sacred Musical Repository* and the Wyeth collection would in itself lead to the suspicion that Boyd knew *Part Second*. This is confirmed through the 13 tunes he borrowed from Wyeth, a selection quite different from that made by Davisson. In the preface to *The Missouri Harmony*, Allen D. Carden "acknowledges himself indebted to Mr. 'Wyeth's Repository, part second' for many of the rules and remarks contained in this introduction"; he was also indebted to Wyeth for 19 tunes. Funk borrowed 11 for his *Genuine Church Music*, despite his professed abhorrence for such "ephemera"; Walker 20 for *The Southern Harmony;* White and King 11 for *The Sacred Harp*. Only the last collection to appear in point of time, the 1844 *Sacred Harp*, does not show conclusive evidence of heavy borrowings specifically from *Part Second*. By that late date, however, it is quite likely that the Wyeth book was no longer a major factor in Southern folk-hymnody, having been supplanted by others, among them the very tune-books it had supplied with distinctive melodic materials.

Many of the folk-hymns which emerged in print for the first time in *Part Second* are to be found in modern anthologies of American folk-hymnody, generally rediscovered in later sources than the Wyeth collection. Table II shows the extent to which the 44 Wyeth folk-hymns appears in five major collections of this sort.

Particularly noteworthy as an indication of the importance of the Wyeth body of folk-hymnody is the comparison with the list of the most popular tunes in the Southern tradition which appears in Jackson's *White Spirituals in the Southern Uplands*. The Jackson list is based on an analysis of 15 Southern tune-books. Of his 80 tunes, 65 fall in the folk-hymn category, and it is significant that 12 of these first appeared in *Part Second*. It is evident that only 28 of the 44 Wyeth folk-hymns are available in these modern anthologies. The remaining 16, which include some excellent examples of the idiom, are unknown except in the pages of *Part Second*.

INTRODUCTION

TABLE II

Tune Name	JWS	JSF	BFH	JDE	JAS	Tune Name	JWS	JSF	BFH	JDE	JAS
Adoration		30				Minister's Farewell	48			18	13
Animation					85	Morality	79			138	
Christmas Hymn			40			New Canaan	26	122			
Communion	57	24				New Monmouth					
Concert					210	Ninety-Third	25		29	146	
Consolation (I)			3	135		Perseverance					
Consolation (II)				131		Power					
Davis			18			Redeeming Grace			14		
Dependence						Restoration					
Dismission						Roadstown				30	
Fairton						Rockbridge	38				204
Fiducia	15		183			Rockingham	29			150	
Forster			66			Solicitude					
Glasgow	56					Solitude				209	
Hallelujah		101				Spring Hill			7	158	
Happiness						Sterling					
Heavenly Union			38	9		Sublimity					
Kedron	71	57				Transport				48	
Landaff				199		Twenty-Fourth	5			165	
Messiah						Unitia					
Middle Paxton						Vernon	49			19	
Millville						Willington					

Key

JWS   George Pullen Jackson, *White Spirituals in the Southern Uplands* (1933)

JSF   George Pullen Jackson, *Spiritual Folk-Songs of Early America* (1937)

BFH   Annabel Morris Buchanan, *Folk Hymns of America* (1938)

JDE   George Pullen Jackson, *Down-East Spirituals and others* (1943)

JAS   George Pullen Jackson, *Another Sheaf of White Spirituals* (1952)

Note: The numbers are those of the folk-hymns as they appear in the various collections. Entries under *JWS* pertain to the list of the 80 most popular tunes in the Southern tradition as found there.

In view of the undeniably important role played by *Part Second* in the beginnings of Southern folk-hymnody, some information about the men who were connected with it and something of the provenance of the collection itself might be useful. Oddly enough, John Wyeth (1770-1858) does not seem to have been a musician, and there is no evidence that he was even particularly interested in music other than from a purely business point of view. Wyeth (whose exciting youthful days included a stay in the island of San Domingo, from whence he escaped in a series of hairbreadth adventures) was a book publisher of some prominence and the editor and printer of *The Oracle of Dauphin,* a weekly Harrisburg newspaper, at the time he began to engage in the publication of tune-books. In all probability, he was attracted to this field because of the financial success of several earlier collections, such as the Little and Smith *Easy Instructor,* Adgate's *Philadelphia Harmony,* the anonymous *Village Harmony,* and Isaiah Thomas's

INTRODUCTION

Worcester Collection. His 1810 *Repository of Sacred Music* was clearly modelled after these tune-books, from all of which he borrowed materials. Wyeth's function as "compiler" seems to have been similar to that of Isaiah Thomas (also a non-musician), who consulted with local musicians of his acquaintance in gauging popular taste and then attempted to cater to it.[8] Wyeth succeeded in hitting the jackpot with the 1810 *Repository*, which is said to have sold 120,000 copies. Its popularity was probably the principal factor in persuading him to continue publishing tune-books.

The idea of *Part Second* no doubt originated in Wyeth's mind as a potentially profitable business venture. The collection was designed to attract Methodist and Baptist groups, who were the singers of folk-hymnody at the time. This was a large and expanding market; the revivalistic fervor and religious enthusiasm then sweeping the country were making many converts, the ranks of the folk-hymn singers were rapidly increasing, and no collection of the sort envisioned by Wyeth was available to them. Wyeth himself had no personal religious inclination in that direction, as he was an extremely active Unitarian.[9]

The fact that Wyeth himself was no musician poses a collateral problem: whose were the *musical* brains behind *Part Second?* It appears highly probable that the person responsible for the organization of the tune-book and its general editorial supervision was the Rev. Elkanah Kelsay Dare (1782-1826), Methodist clergyman, Freemason, and musician, who at one time served as the dean of boys at Wilmington College, Wilmington, Del., an institution long since defunct. Dare was the author of a theoretical work on music, quoted at some length in the introduction to *Part Second*, which apparently never achieved publication.[10] He is represented as a composer in the Wyeth collection by 13 tunes (all published for the first time), the largest number credited to any single individual in *Part Second*. It is logical to assume that Dare was perhaps charged with the responsibility of notating and arranging the 30 unattributed tunes newly published in the tune-book, but this should not preclude the possibility that one of the others associated with Wyeth may have performed this task. So far as it has been ascertained, *Part Second* is the only tune-book to which Dare personally contributed; all the tunes attributed to him in later collections can be traced to this original source. If Dare was the main musical figure behind *Part Second*, he must be considered most important in the foundation of the Southern singing tradition, and hence is undoubtedly entitled to at least a footnote in the history of American music.

Another little known, but nevertheless important name which comes to light for the first time in *Part Second* is that of "Chapin," to whom seven tunes were attributed. Several of these (as well as some of Dare's tunes) are to be found in the Jackson list of the most popular tunes in the Southern tradition cited earlier. But despite the fact that music by "Chapin" is

---

[8] Frank J. Metcalf's attribution to Wyeth of the well known hymn-tune "Nettleton" (first published without composer attribution as "Hallelujah" in *Part Second*) is questionable. This claim is found in *Stories of Hymn Tunes* (New York, 1928).

[9] Other examples of Wyeth's adventurous opportunism in tune-book publication are known. He attempted to tap the German-speaking Pennsylvania market with two most interesting collections, Joseph Doll's *Der leichte Unterricht* (Harrisburg, Pa., 1810) and Johannes Rothbaust's *Die Franklin Harmonie* (Harrisburg, Pa., 1821), both of which exhibit a most remarkable cross-blend of all sorts of different cultural trends in American music—and both of which also derive from *The Easy Instructor*.

[10] See page 3 of *Part Second*, where Wyeth writes: "The following observations on Music, are extracted, by permission, from the Manusript [*sic*] work of E. K. DARE, A. B. late of Wilmington college, which we hope, ere long to see published entire." Perhaps Dare submitted the manuscript to Wyeth for publication and thus came to his attention as a musician. If the book was published it seems to have completely disappeared; I have been able to locate no other mention of it.

found in many Southern compilations, the identity of the composer remains something of a minor mystery. In all probability, he was one Lucius Chapin (1760-1842), a Massachusettsian who enlisted as a fifer in the Revolutionary War and went into the Shenandoah Valley of Virginia as a practiced singing-master as early as 1787.[11]

Interestingly enough, Chapin appears to

[11] See Charles Hamm, "The Chapins and Sacred Music in the South and West," *Journal of Research in Music Education*, VIII, 2 (Fall 1960), 91-98. Both "L. Chapin" and "A. Chapin" are frequently cited in Southern tune-books, the latter being Lucius' brother Amzi Chapin (1768-1835), also a singing-master. Hamm points out that Amzi joined Lucius in Virginia in 1791, and feels that Ananias Davisson probably received his instruction in music from one or both of the Chapins. He also demonstrates that the confusion about the identity of the Chapin who composed the folk-hymns is perhaps a bit more complex than was previously suspected, since no fewer than seven Chapins (six of them from the Lucius-Amzi Chapin family) were involved in music at the time. Confusion has been worse confounded, thanks to Joe S. James, editor of the "historical" edition of the White and King *Sacred Harp* published in Atlanta under the title, *The Original Sacred Harp*, as late as 1929. Mr. James manages to get Chapin mixed up with that well-known composer of American folk-hymns, F. F. Chopin! This is forgivable in a work which can be considered at best one of "folk musicology," but what is one to say about John Jacob Niles's *Shape-Note Study Book* (New York, 1950), where "Chapin" becomes Amzi Chopin?

TABLE III

Composer	Number of Tunes	Composer	Number of Tunes
Anonymous	38	*Hibbert	1
Madan	10	*Holyoke	1
*Billings	9	*Ingalls	1
*Kimball	3	Kirby	1
*Holden	3	Lane	1
*Brown	2	*Morgan	1
*Bull	2	*Peck	1
*Selby	2	Pleyel	1
Tans'ur	2	Premmer	1
Arne	1	*Read	1
*Doolittle	1	Shrubsole	1
*French	1	*Shumway	1
*Gillet	1	Smith	1
*Hall	1	*Wood	1
Handel	1		

Note: American composers are asterisked.

have been associated with Davisson as well as with Wyeth, and several Chapin tunes were published for the first time in the *Kentucky Harmony*. This Chapin may well have been the person responsible for introducing *Part Second* to the Southern compiler.

Still another name found in *Part Second* establishing a connection between Wyeth and Davisson is that of White, who probably was the same "White" with whom Davisson collaborated in the composition of a few tunes first published in *The Supplement to the Kentucky Harmony* (Harrisonburg, Va., 1820). An Austin is known to have contributed to Stephen Jenks's *Delights of Harmony, or Norfolk Compiler* (Dedham, Mass., 1805), and M. Kyes to Asahel Benham's *Social Harmony* (Wallingford, Conn., 1798). Of the others to whom new tunes are attributed in *Part Second* (Robison or Robinson,[12] Findlay, Lewer, and C. Curtis), nothing at all is known.

Some attempt also has been made to trace

[12] Alternative spellings from the 1st and 2nd editions of *Part Second*.

the backgrounds of *Part Second* from the tunes found in its pages which were borrowed from previous printed sources. These are 91 in number, and Table III shows the composers to whom they are attributed.

Discounting the 38 tunes which appear without composer attribution (most of which are, nevertheless, clearly of American origin), 33 of the remaining 51 are by Americans. Of the 91 old tunes, 28 are fuging-tunes; from these, some of the exact tune-books used by Wyeth in compiling *Part Second* can be identified. His sources include Daniel Read's *Columbian Harmonist* (Boston, 1807; 3rd edition), the Little and Smith *Easy Instructor* (Albany, N. Y.; an edition published between 1809 and 1811), Isaiah Thomas's *Worcester Collection* (Boston; one of the editions edited by Oliver Holden between 1797 and 1803, either the 6th, 7th, or 8th), Ebenezer Child's *Sacred Musician* (Boston, 1804), Thomas H. Atwill's *New York and Vermont Collection* (both the 1st edition, Lansingburgh, N. Y., 1802, and the 2nd edition, Albany, N. Y., 1804), and the anonymous *Village Harmony* (Exeter, N. H.; either the 5th edition of 1800, the 6th of 1803, or the 7th of 1806). Others were unquestionably utilized, but it is impossible to establish their identity conclusively.

Even in such a strikingly homegrown collection of American music as is *Part Second*, the growing English influence which was driving the native music out of the urban centers is evident. Ten tunes attributed to Martin Madan, the English compiler of *The Lock Hospital Collection* (probably reprinted from other American sources, however) were included by Wyeth. This was actually a greater number than he printed by William Billings, a forecast of the coming victory of European church song and its American advocates.

Our folk-hymnody is, of course, significant as a written record of the exact state of the American singing tradition in the first half of the 19th century, but completely aside from its historical interest, it is a body of music of great individuality, genuine merit, and melodic charm. It is possibly the most valuable musical heritage that has come down to us from early American times. We are becoming increasingly aware of this, and we surely owe a debt of gratitude to George Pullen Jackson who, almost unaided by other scholars, brought this music to light. Those unworked mines of early American music, the so-called "long-boys" or "end-openers," as they are descriptively nicknamed, offer a surprisingly fertile field for investigation by students of our music history. John Wyeth's *Repository of Sacred Music, Part Second* is only one of hundreds of tunebooks containing (as well as folk-hymns) thousands of compositions by early American composers in a unique and little understood harmonic and melodic idiom. They have been unaccountably neglected, despite the fact that as primary sources of the first magnitude, they are essential to a full understanding and an accurate reconstruction of 18th- and early 19th-century American musical life. These collections of tunes are repositories of a vital and interesting music; they are also the raw materials for pages of an as yet unwritten history of American music. May this facsimile of *Part Second*[13] call to the attention of the world of scholarship one of the most influential and consequential examples of the genre.

IRVING LOWENS
WASHINGTON, D. C.

---

[13] The second edition of *Part Second* has been utilized as prototype because, although the musical and textual content is virtually identical, the publisher or the compiler took advantage of the reissue to correct some of the misprints to be found in the first edition. It should not, however, therefore be assumed that the second edition is entirely free from errors.

NOTE: This preface is, in effect, a considerably revised version of an article by me which was published in the Summer 1952 issue of the *Journal of the American Musicological Society*. Permission to reprint and alter the article was generously given by the Society, and it appears here in a form which should be understood to supersede the original.   I. L.

A POSTSCRIPT ON SHAPE-NOTES

Since Wyeth's *Part Second* makes use of shape notation, a few sentences of history and explanation might prove helpful to those who are unfamiliar with this particular application of Yankee ingenuity to the ancient problem (and one whose difficulties puzzle us still) of how to teach successfully the core skill of reading music at sight.

The approach through notational reform, considered hopelessly quixotic today, came in for a good deal of attention in 18th- and early 19th-century America. Indeed, the first music textbook published on this side of the Atlantic, John Tufts's *An Introduction to the Singing of Psalm-Tunes* (Boston, 1721), presented an innovation which was no doubt of some value in a situation where the art of reading orthodox notation had virtually disappeared. The nub of the problem was to devise a system in which pitch, time, and solmization were combined into a single, easily assimilated notation. The Tufts solution was to abandon ordinary notes entirely and to substitute upon the staff the initial letters of the four solmization syllables (fa, sol, la, mi) then in universal use in Great Britain. Time values were indicated with punctuation marks. This was quite adequate for the traditional psalm-tunes Tufts included in his clearly written and unpretentious little pamphlet, but the system was unwieldy and ill-adapted to music of greater complexity. It failed to win adherents, although the *Introduction* itself proved to be something of a best seller, going through eleven editions.

Among the ingenious notations which followed in the wake of the Tufts experiment, none was more remarkable than the "shape-note" system which made its first public appearance in 1801 on the pages of a quite extraordinary tune-book, *The Easy Instructor*, "by" William Little and William Smith. The shape-note idea was a kind of inspired solution to a knotty problem—a solution which seems perfectly obvious once it has been suggested. It consisted merely of using a differently shaped note-head to represent each of the four syllables. Thus, a triangular note-head represented fa, a round note-head sol, a square note-head la, and a diamond note-head mi. In all other respects the notation was completely orthodox.

The clear advantages of the shape-note system are almost immediately apparent. Providing an individual shape for each syllable enables anyone, after a modicum of attention to the matter, to name the proper syllables of any piece of music instantaneously. One of the genuine difficulties in ordinary solmization lies in the fact that keys change and hence do (or fa in the fasola system) does not remain in the same place. The student must make continual mental computations. With shape-notes, this is completely avoided. A somewhat subtler advantage is that the shapes are continually before the singer whether he happens to be singing words or syllables. Thus, the true function of any solmization system—that of aiding in the automatic identification of scale degrees—is emphasized and capitalized upon through shape-notes in a fashion impossible in any system which permits abandonment of the process of syllabification when words are sung. Comparison of the shape-note system with that of Tonic Sol-Fa, so successful in the British Isles, highlights the superiority of the *Easy Instructor* idea. The symbols of Tonic Sol-Fa are not posited upon a staff, and hence the pictorial suggestion of tonal direction provided by staff notation is lost. Failure to use the staff demands a complicated method of octave identification, and failure to use regular notes demands a similarly complicated method of representing time values. Furthermore, Tonic Sol-Fa is quite independent of orthodox notation, whereas the shape-notes utilize the standard notation and add to it a graphic, quickly comprehended key to relative scale degrees.

No one who has witnessed the astonishing sight-singing virtuosity exhibited by the shape-note singers of the rural South today, trained with what is basically the *Easy Instructor* method, can possibly doubt the effectiveness of the device. Had this pedagogical tool been accepted by "the father of singing among the children," Lowell Mason, and others who shaped the patterns of American music education, we might have been more successful in developing skilled music readers and enthusiastic amateur choral singers in the public schools. The reasons for the rejection of shape-notes — Thomas Hastings, one of their most vociferous early detractors, called them "dunce notes"—had nothing to do with the system's merits or demerits. The shape-notes from their very inception were closely associated with music in the New England idiom and folk-hymnody. The "reformers" who quickly arose in earnest protest against this first flowering of American musical expression, all too conscious of the European musical tradition and possessed of an inferiority complex regarding peculiarly American cultural manifestations, eventually saw to the elimination of this music from American life, at least in the North. In the meantime, the shape-note system and the music itself became completely identified. Shape-notes came to be regarded in urban centers as the musical notation of the country people, the naive, simple people who sang for their own enjoyment songs in an odd, almost primitive native idiom. Leaders of fine city choirs busy with Pucitta and Neukomm (as well as Handel and Haydn) would have nothing to do with such music nor with such notation. Inevitably the city choir leaders became the first music teachers in the public schools. Shape-notes were never admitted to the regular classroom. As a result, the child who learns music in our schools today must do so without the aid that they might give.*

I. L.

---

*Dr. George H. Kyme of the University of California succeeded in demonstrating the superiority of a seven-shape notation over orthodox notation as a device for teaching sight-singing during the course of an ingenious controlled experiment, carried out in 1955-56, involving 183 fourth- and fifth-grade pupils in the San Francisco Bay area. For a report of his findings, see "An Experiment in Teaching Children to Read Music with Shape Notes," *Journal of Research in Music Education*, VIII, 1 (Spring 1960), 3-8.

WYETH's
REPOSITORY OF SACRED MUSIC.

PART SECOND.——(2d. Edition.)

ORIGINAL AND SELECTED FROM THE MOST EMINENT AND APPROVED AUTHORS IN THAT SCIENCE.

FOR THE USE OF

CHRISTIAN CHURCHES, SINGING-SCHOOLS & PRIVATE SOCIETIES.

TOGETHER WITH A PLAIN AND CONCISE

INTRODUCTION TO THE GROUNDS OF MUSIC,
AND RULES FOR LEARNERS.

By *JOHN WYETH.*

PRINTED (typographically) at HARRISBURGH, Penn. by JOHN WYETH, Printer and Bookseller, and sold by him, and by most of the Booksellers in Philadelphia; SHAEFFER & MAUND, Baltimore, and COLLINS & Co. New-York. Either of whom will give a liberal allowance to wholesale purchasers.

1820.

DISTRICT OF PENNSYLVANIA, to wit:

BE it remembered, That on the *twenty-eighth* day of *April,* in the thirty-seventh year of the independence of the United States of America, A. D. 1813, JOHN WYETH, of the said district, hath deposited in this office, the title of a book, the right whereof he claims as proprietor, in the words following, to wit.

WYETH's Repository of Sacred Music. Part Second. Original and selected from the most eminent and approved authors in that science, for the use of Christian Churches, Singing Schools and private Societies. Together with a copious and plain Introduction to the Grounds of Music, and Rules for Learners. By JOHN WYETH."

In conformity to the act of the congress of the United States, Intituled, "An act for the encouragement of learning by securing the copies of maps, charts and books, to the authors and proprietors of such copies during the times therein mentioned." And also to the act entitled, "An act supplementary to an act, entitled, "An act for the encouragement of learning by securing the copies of maps, charts, and books, to the authors and proprietors of such copies during the times therein mentioned," and extending the benefits thereof to the arts of designing, engraving, and etching historical and other prints.

D. CALDWELL, *Clerk of the District of Pennsylvania.*

☞ *THE editor and compiler of this volume, cannot refrain from acknowledging, with gratitude, the very flattering manner which the several editions of his Repository have been received by the public. While introducing this second part, he by no means wishes it to be understood, that the first is to be laid aside;* **its continued and increasing patronage forbids it; yet, he is well aware, that however pleasing that or any other collection may be, the lover of music can never be satiated so long as the heavenly science can be susceptible of extending its variety. The editor has introduced copious rules, so that either collection may be complete and satisfactory to schools and societies.*

**A supply may always be had at the usual places. A 5th edition improved has lately been published.*

☞ *It cannot be supposed that the few following pages will contain all that might be said on the subject of which they treat.—Persons desirous of a more perfect knowledge of Music than these pages can afford, are referred to the British Encyclopedia, Dr. Rees's Cyclopedia, Anarcharsis (the younger's) travels through Greece, &c. &c. They will there see the subject treated at large under its proper heads. The following observations on Music, are extracted, by permission, from the Manuscript work of E. K. Dare, A. B. late of Wilmington college, which we hope, ere long to see published entire.*

On the Genera of Music. *From Dr.* Rees's Cyclopedia—*with Additions.*

HISTORY informs us that the Greeks included all musical sounds in three *genera*, or kinds of intervals viz. the DIATONIC for tones and semitones; the CHROMATIC for semitones, and minor thirds; and the ENHARMONIC for quarter tones and major thirds. The scale of each genus was arranged in tetrachords or systems of four sounds, of which the first and last were stantes, that is *immobiles* or fixed; while the two middle sounds were termed *mobiles* or changeable, and it is by these changes that the *genera* are distinguished.

Each of the three *genera* had some sound in its scale, that were peculiar and characteristic, and some that were in common with the other two. For instance, B C E F A B and D, were used in all three *genera*, whereas D and G were peculiar to the Diatonic; C♯ and F♯ to the Chromatic; and Bx Ex and Ax to the *Enharmonic*.

As the character used after B E and A (viz. x) in the preceding line, being in little use, at present, I have thought proper to give its definition.

The *diesis* x (for so it is called) in *ancient music*, was the *Enharmonic* sharp— in *modern* Italian music, it implies a common ♯, or minor semitone. The Enharmonic sharp (*or quarter tone*) in the Greek, is used in modern music for a double sharp; as in a key with many sharps at the cliff, if it is necessary to elevate one of the sounds (already sharped) a nominal semitone, it is, or should be expressed by an Enharmonic *diesis* (x).—It is said that the French and Italians have no other word to express a sharp or minor semitone, than *dieze or diesis.*——It is used in these observations on the genera of music, only as a *quarter tone*. Having given this definition, I proceed.

As modern melody is built upon harmony, derived from the harmonies of the fundamental bass, we have no instruments with *quarter tones*, or which can furnish a bass to an Enharmonic melody, if we had the power of forming and executing it with the voice or violin. We have, therefore, only *two genera* in our music, with all our refinements in melody of nominal Enharmonic sharps, diesis, double flats, sharps, &c. which two genera, viz. the *Diatonic*, consisting of five tones and two semitones in an octave, such as the key of C natural supplies, upon keyed instruments, and such as the natural scale *we have* in general use; & the *Chromatic*, consisting of semitones, twelve in number, such as moving from any given note to its octave by semitones will furnish.

In modern music, as before observed, the genera are only two, viz. the Diatonic & Chromatic. These consist in the manner of arranging the tones & semitones of which melody is composed. Indeed the chromatic music in use, at present, can hardly be compared with that of the ancients—for with *them* every accidental flat or sharp which led to a new Key or mode, would have been called a *change of genus*. With *us*, however, a mere change of modulation, though it occasions a *change of key* is not a change of genus; for while the sounds used in harmony and melody can be referred to any one key, the Diatonic genus is supposed to be preserved.

We have numerous instances of the key and mode being changed in the *same* tune or piece of music. The "Dying Christian" commences on F *minor* mode, and soon changes to F *major*; The "Judgment Anthem" contains various changes of mode and key, and yet we may pronounce them, and similar tunes to be comprised in the Diatonic genus or scale.

In the Diatonic genus, the melody proceeded by a semitone and two tones, as from B to C a semitone; from C to D a tone, and from D to E a tone.

The Chromatic genus proceeded by two successive semitones and a hemiditone (that is a minor 3d) as from B to C a semitone; from C to C# a semitone, and from C# to E a tone & a half, or minor 3d.

The *Enharmonic* tetrachord proceeded by two quarter tones and a major 3d, as from B to Bx (*diesis*) a quarter tone; from Bx to C a quarter tone (the natural intervals between B and C being a semitone) and from C to E, two tones or a major 3d.

Having made these general, but brief remarks upon the three genera of music, (two of which having ceased to be in use with us) I shall now confine myself to the Diatonic, and exhibit the same, on the following staves.

The Diatonic Scale of the Greeks.

This genus, it was noticed, proceeded by a semitone and two tones, as B C D E, the semitone lying between B and C (and is indicated by a star in the above stave) the whole tones, between C and D and D and E as indicated by the white notes. The *fourth* being the constant boundary of sounds in ancient music (as the octave is that in the modern) we may suppose the above stave to exhibit the Diatonic genus.—But when we proceed to enlarge upon this tetrachord, or system of four sounds, we project such a scale as is now in use, viz.

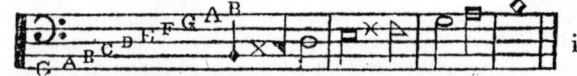

Thus we have a scale of five whole and two semitones to an octave; the natural place of the semitones being between B and C and E and F.

Having thus briefly treated on the genera of music, I proceed to make some observations on the rules of harmony &c. first observing, that agreeably to the general acceptation of the term *melody*, it means a pleasing succession of musical sounds without regard, or accompanied with, any chord—or more simply speaking, melody is the air or leading part of a correct tune performed alone—& *harmony* is a combination of sounds arranged agreeably to the rules of concord—or, harmony means the parts of a correct tune performed at the same time.

On the Intervals in Music.

The distance (says Mr. Boyd and others) between any two notes, whether remote or immediate, is called an *interval*. These intervals are called tones semitones, thirds, fifths, &c. which I will endeavor to explain in regular order.

It is universally agreed by authors, in our day, that an octave (or eighth of music) contains five whole & two semitones, that sounds naturally succeed each other in music, ascending from the first (that is admitting C to be the key note, or any other letter substituted for the key of the major mode) to the second, a tone, from the second to the third, a tone; from the third to the fourth, a semitone; from the fourth to the fifth, a tone; from the fith to the sixth, a tone; from the sixth to the seventh, a tone, and from the seventh to the eighth, a semitone. But when reckoning from the key note of the minor mode, the semitones lie between the second, and third, and fifth, and sixth, instead of between the third and fourth, and seventh and eighth of the major mode; wherefore this order of tones and semitones is called the *NATURAL SCALE OF MUSIC**—as follows.

The Gamut; or, General Scale.

22				ALT. G space above.	sol
21				F—5th—line	faw
20				E* 4th space.	law
19				D—4th-line	sol
18				C 3d space.	faw
17			B*	3d—line—MI	mi
16			A	2d space.	law
15		space above. G	TREBLE STAV	2d—line	sol
14		F—5th—line		1st space.	faw
13		E* 4th space.		1st-line-of-*Treble-stave*	law
12		D—4th—line			sol
11		C 3d space.	TENOR STAVE		faw
10	space above.	B*—3d—line—MI			mi
9	5th—line	A 2d space.			law
8	4th space.	G 2d—line			sol
7	4th—line	F 1st space.			faw
6	3d space.	E*; 1st-—line-of-*Tenor-stave*			law
5	3d—line	D			sol
4	2d space.	C* Natural Key note of the Major mode			faw
3	2d—line	B			mi
2	1st space. A	Natural Key note of the Minor mode			law
1	1st—line-G--of--the—*Bass*				sol

* Guido, an Italian monk, it is said, invented this scale, about the year A. D. 1022. It has been improved since his time.

A 2

The foregoing scale comprises three octaves, or 22 sounds. The F Cliff, 𝄢 used on the 4th line in the Bass, shews that that line is the 7th sound in the general scale   The G Cliff 𝄞 used on the second line in the Tenor and   Treble, shows that that line in the Tenor is the 8th sound in the general scale. and in the Treble the 15th sound.   The stars,* show the natural places of the semitones.

By attending to the preceding scale the order of tones and semitones will appear to be as above stated.

Three octaves (observes Mr. Adgate and others) being more than any common voice can perform, we therefore, assign the bass to the gravest of men's voices—the tenor to the highest of men's, and the treble to female voices; the counter *when used* to boys—It is now however (and I think justly) customary to assign the air or leading part of the tune to the females—but this does not destroy the scale, as the interval between a woman and a man's voice is an octave, the former being an octave more acute than the latter.

Let the tenor or air of a tune be performed by the ladies, and it places that stave in the usual place for the stave of treble—then the next part below is callled a second, & the lower one the bass. This method of writing music is now in great vogue. But to return to the intervals. Two sounds equally high or equally low, however unequal in their force, are said to be in *unison* one with the other. Consequently E on the lower line in the treble stave is in *unison* with E on the fourth space in the tenor; and E on the third space in the bass is in *unison* with E on the lower line of the tenor, and an octave below E on the lower line in the treble. ☞ See the general scale.

From any one letter in the general scale to another of the same name, the interval is an octave—thus as from B to B, D to D, E to E, &c.

Agreeably to the F and G cliffs used in the general scale, a note on any line or space in the bass is a 6th below a note on a corresponding line or space in the tenor, and a 13th below a note in the treble occupying the same line or space. Suppose we place a note on D, middle line of the bass, another on B middle line of the tenor and treble, the interval will appear as just stated: and to find any other interval, count either ascending or descending as the case may be.

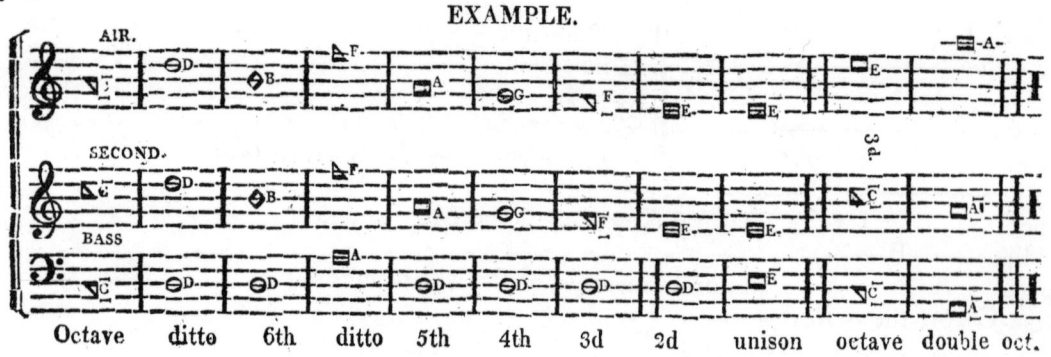

EXAMPLE.

Octave   ditto   6th   ditto   5th   4th   3d   2d   unison   octave   double oct.

In counting intervals, remember to *include* both notes or letters; thus as in counting a 6th in the above example, D is one, E is two, F is three, G is four, A is five, and B is 6 &c.

When the C Cliff is used, the middle line in the counter is in *unison* with the 3d space in the tenor, (C) and a 7th above the middle line in the bass, &c.

In the above example, the notes in the *air* and second are placed in unison with each other. But by assigning the *air* to female voices and the *second* to men's, an octave must be added to the notes in the air, (as previously observed of a woman's voice being an octave more acute than a man's) the interval then between the bass and air, in the first part would be a 15th or double octave, in the third bar, the note on B in the air, a 13th above D in the bass, &c.

It must be observed likewise that an octave and a second make a 9th; an octave and a third, make a 10th; an octave and a fourth a 11th; an octave & a fifth, a 12th; an octave & a sixth, a 13th; an octave & a seventh, a 14th; two octaves a 15th, &c. always *including* the first and last notes.

When a ledger line is added to the treble stave, a note occupying it is said to be in *alt*, and when notes descend below the bass stave, they are termed *doubles*.

Terms by which the different *intervals* in the *Gamut* are denominated.

1. An interval composed of a tone and a semitone, as from *mi* to *sol*, that is, from B to D, is called a minor 3d.

2. An interval composed of two full tones, as from *faw* to *law*, i. e. from C to E, is called a third major.

3. An interval composed of two tones and a semitone, as from *mi* to *law*, i. e. from B to E, is called a fourth.

4. An interval composed of three full tones, as from *faw* to *mi*, i. e. from F to B is called triton, or 4th redundant.

8

5 An interval composed of three tones and a semitone, as from *faw* to *sol*, i. e. from C to G, or from G to D, is called a fifth.

6 An interval composed of three tones and two semitones, as from *law* to *faw*, i. e. from E to C, is called a sixth minor.

7 An interval composed of four tones and a semitone, as from *faw* to *law* i. e. from C to A, is called a sixth major.

8 An interval composed of four tones and two semitones, as from *sol* to *faw*, i. e. from D to C, is called a seventh minor. [See in next example.]

9 An interval composed of five tones and a semitone, as from *faw* to *mi*, i. e. from C to B, is called a seventh major.

10 An interval composed of five tones and two semitones (as already observed) is called an octave. *Example of the three last mentioned intervals.*

The preceding intervals are counted ascending or upwards, and the star indicates the place and number of semitones in each example. *Note.* It may be particularly remembered that the semitones *always* lie between *mi* and *faw*, and *law* and *faw*.

Of Harmony.

Having given an explanation of the different intervals contained in the octave, I proceed to show how they may be used to produce harmony.

Harmony consists (says Mr. Boyd) in the proportion of the distance of four sounds performed at the same instant of time, and mingling in a most pleasing manner to the ear. The British Encyclopedia says *two* or more sounds. I feel willing to subscribe to both—the former comprizing what I should term *full* harmony, and the latter *partial*.

The notes which produce harmony, when sounded together are called *concords*, and their intervals, *consonant intervals*—The notes, which when sounded together, produce a disagreeable sound to the ear, are called *discords*, and their intervals *dissonant intervals*.

There are but four *Concords* in music, viz. *Unison*, *Third*, *Fifth*, and *Sixth*, (their eights or octaves are also meant.) The unison is called a *perfect chord*, and commonly the Fifth is so called, but the Fifth may be made *imperfect*, if the composer pleases. The Third and Sixth are called *imperfect*; their chords not being so full, nor so agreeable to the ear, as the *perfect*; but in four parts, the Sixth is often used instead of the fifth, in some certain places when the Fifth is left out; so in effect there are but three *Concords*, employed together, in composition.

N. B. The meaning of *imperfect*, signifies that it wants a semitone of its *perfection*, to what it does when it is perfect; for, as the lesser, or imperfect Third, includes but three half tones; the greater or major Third, includes four half tones, &c.

The *Discords* are a *Second* a *Fourth*, and a *Seventh*, and their octaves; though sometimes the greater fourth comes very near to the sound of an imperfect chord, it being the same in ratio as the minor Fifth. The following is an example of the several Concords & Discords, with their octaves under them.

	CONCORDS.	DISCORDS.
Single Chords—	1. 3. 5. 6.	2. 4. 7.
Their octaves	8. 10. 12. 13.	9. 11. 14.
	15. 17. 19. 20.	16. 18. 21.
	22. 24. 26. 27.	23. 25. 28.

Notwithstanding the 2nd, 4th, 7th, 9th, &c. produce properly discords, yet they may be used to advantage in composition. Many authors seem partial to them. In the celebrated tune "Denmark" written by Dr. Madan, several dissonant chords may be found. However, whenever they are used they should be immediately followed by a perfect chord. They will then answer a similar purpose to *acid*, which being tasted immediately previous to *sweet* gives the latter a more pleasing flavor.

As the rules for preparing discords are very lengthy, the inquisitive are referred to them in the Cyclopedia &c.

I will annex a couple examples which will give some light on the subject—the first of which is selected from the tune Hotham written by the same author as Denmark, wherein a *third* and a *fourth* are mixed with a *second* to advantage. The 3d notes from the cliff are referred to. The other example is selected from the tune "Dismission" inserted in this collection of music, the 9th bar from the cliff.

In the first bar of the these examples, the note in the *air*, that is, upper stave, is one tone higher, (which is a 2d) than the note in the second stave; and a minor or flat 3d below the note in the bass. As B is flatted at the cliff, the interval between it and G, is one tone and a semitone, instead of two tones, the natural interval. This makes the minor 3d. The interval between the note in the bass and the one in the second stave on F, is a 4th; that is, two tones and a semitone.

In the bar selected from Dismission, the note in the *air* or upper stave, is a minor third below the note on C in the second stave, and a fifth above the note on D in the bass, consequently they produce harmony—the interval between the note in the second stave, and the one in the bass is a minor seventh, (*discord*.) But suppose we place a choosing note on F in the bass; the interval will then be between it and the one in the *air*, a 3d between it and the one in the second stave a 5th—and between it and the one on D in the bass, a 3d, all consonant intervals.

These observations being made, we may suppose that when we can arrange notes in such a manner as to produce *two* consonants to *one* dissonant chord, the laws of harmony are not greatly violated.

The 4th within itself produces a *discord*—but let a female voice sound a note a 4th below one sounded by a man's in the general scale; and by reason of her voice being an octave more acute than his, it *raises* the 4th to a 5th above the note sounded by the man's voice.

The first bar exhibits the fourth as written; the second bar exhibits the same, as sounded by a female voice. To prove this let a man sound the high G and a woman the low G, they will discover that the sounds are in *unison* with each other.

It may be noticed that a 4th and a 5th make an octave. Likewise a 6th and a third—and that two *thirds* make a 5th. Consequently if a 4th is used over a 5th they will produce perfect harmony. Let the following example suffice.

The interval in the first bar between the note on G, in the upper stave, & C in the second stave, is a 4th; and between it & C in the bass, a 5th, which produce an octave. In the second bar, the interval between E in the upper stave and C in the second stave is a third; and between C in the second stave, and E in the bass, a 6th, which make an octave. In the third bar, the interval between D in the upper stave, and B in the second stave, is a 3d; and the interval between B in the second stave and G in the bass, is a 3d, which make a 5th between G and D.

On the *Key Notes* in *Music*.

There are, in reality, only two key notes in music, viz. the key of the major mode *faw*, and the key of the minor mode *law*. The Key note is always found, (in a correct tune) in the last bar of the bass, and is either the first note above or below *mi*.

The key note of the major mode has a *major* 3d, 6th and 7th rising above it; & the Key note of the minor mode has a minor 3d, 6th & 7th, rising above it. The former key generally, produces sprightly music—and the latter pensive. Therefore words which are used in psalms of praise, such as "Exalt the Lord our God," should be set to the major key; and words which are used in psalms of petitioning, &c. such as "Come, holy spirit, heav'nly dove," should be set to the minor Key.

EXAMPLE OF THE KEYS.

In the major mode from *faw* to *law*, its 3d, the interval is two tones [a major 3d] from *faw* to *law* its 6th, the interval is four tones and a semitone [a major 6th]—and from *faw* to *mi*, its seventh, the interval is five tones and a semitone [a major 7th.]

In the minor mode, from *law* to *faw*, its third, the interval is one tone and a semitone [minor third] from *law* to *law*, its sixth the interval is three tones and two semitones, [a minor 6th] and from *law* to *sol*, its 7th, the interval is four tones and two semitones, [a minor 7th.]

Although C is the natural letter for the major key, and A that of the minor, it often becomes absolutely necessary to remove the key, which is done by aid of flats and sharps.

To prove the utility of removing the key, I will produce one example, which I think will suffice. Let the tune "Amherst" be written on key note C instead of G, its proper key, and few voices would be able to perform it; thus, The tenor of Amherst on G its proper key, from the repeat.

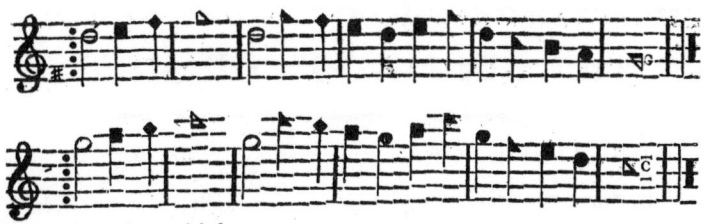

The same on C the assumed key.

Here the notes run on a second ledger line, and a 4th too high.
The want of room compels me to close these extracts or I should feel a signal pleasure in pursuing the subject—Before I close, however, I will observe that the *mi*, and consequently the keys, is removed by either sharping its 5th or flatting its fourth, thus:

Sharp Key.
1. A 5th from B *mi* its natural place, will bring us to   F
2. A 5th from F *mi* will bring us to   C
3. A 5th from C *mi* will bring us to   G
4. A 5th from G *mi* will bring us to   D
5. A 5th from D *mi* will bring us to   A
6. A 5th from A *mi* will bring us to   E
7. A 5th from E *mi* will bring us back to   B

       Which must be sharped.

Flat Key.
1. A 4th from B *mi* will bring us to   E
2. A 4th from E *mi* will bring us to   A
3. A 4th from A *mi* will bring us to   D
4. A 4th from D *mi* will bring us to   G
5. A 4th from G *mi* will bring us to   C
6. A 4th from C *mi* will bring us to   F
7. A 4th from F *mi* will bring us home to   B

       Which must be flatted.

"*By flats the mi is driven round;*
Till forc'd on B to stand its ground:
By sharps the mi's led through the keys,
Till brought to B its native place."

THE RUDIMENTS OF MUSIC.

THERE are seven sounds belonging to every key note in music, which are expressed by the seven first letters of the alphabet, A B C D E F G.

Music is written on five parallel lines, called a Stave, calculated to express the degrees or gradations of sound.

Bass	Tenor	Counter	Treble
Space above — B	G	A	G
Fifth line — A	F	G	F
Fourth Space — G	E	F	E
Fourth line — F	D	E	D
Third space — E	C	D	C
Third line — D	B	C	B
Second Space — C	A	B	A
Second line — B	G	A	G
First space — A	F	G	F
First line — G	E	F	E

Note, a cliff is a character placed at the beginning of every tune, and is considered as a key to open the scale of characters, and fully determines their import. The order of the letters is always the same proceeding from the cliff.

☞ The cliff (or clef) derives its name from two latin words *clavis signata* signifying a sealed key.

This character is called the F Cliff which heretofore has been used only in the Bass, but in this collection, it will sometimes be found on the Counter, for the purpose of bringing the music in the stave.

This character is called the G Cliff, it is used always in the Tenor & Treble, and often in the Counter.

This character is called the C Cliff, and now only used in the Counter.

A single Bar divides the time agreeably to the measure.

A double Bar shows the end of a strain.

A hold ⌒ over a note shows that it must be held somewhat longer than usual.

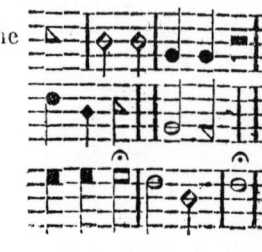

A Flat ♭ set before a note, sinks it half a tone; & when placed at the beginning of a tune, all the notes found on the same line or space, must likewise be sounded half a tone lower.

A ♯ Sharp operates in every instance exactly the reverse of the flat, by raising the note half a tone.

A Natural ♮ restores a note to its primitime sound.

A ledger line — is added when a note ascends or descends a line beyond the stave.

A Slur ⌢ over or under a number of notes or if joined together at bottom, are to be sung to one syllable.

A repeat ⁝ shows that the tune is to be sung twice from the note ⁝ before which it is placed, to the next double bar, or ⁝ close.

A Dot . at the right hand of a note, makes it one half longer.

A Stacato ꞏ implies distinct pronunciation.

A figure 3 over or under any three notes of the same kind, shows that they must be performed in the time of two without a figure.

The figures 1 2 at the end of a strain that is repeated, show that the note or notes under 1, are to be sung before the repeat, and those under 2, after omitting the notes under one; but if tied with a slur, both are to be sung at the repetition.

The Appogiature, or Notes of transition, are small notes added to the regular notes, to guide the voice more easily & gracefully into the sound of the succeeding notes.

A Close ‖ shows the end of a tune.

Moods of Common Time.

The first mood is known by a plain C and has a Semibreve, or its quantity in a measure, sung in the time of four seconds, four beats in a bar, two down and two up.

The second mood is known by a C with a stroke thro it, has the same measure, sung in the time of three seconds, four beats in a bar, two down and two up.

The third mood is known by C inverted, sometimes with a stroke thro it, has the same measure sung in the time of two seconds, has two beats in a bar, one down and the other up.

The fourth mood is known by figure 2 over a figure 3, has a Minim for its measure note, sung in the time of one second, two beats in a bar, one down and the other up.

Modes of *Triple Time*.

The first mode of Triple time is known by a figure 3 over figure 2, has three Minims in a measure, sung in the time of three seconds, three beats in a bar, two down and one up.

The second mode is known by a figure 3 over 4, has three crotchets in a measure, sung as quick again as the first mode, three beats in a bar, two down and one up.

The third mode is known by a figure 3 over an 8, has three quavers in a measure, and sung to the time of the second mode, three beats in a bar, two down and one up.

Modes of Compound Time.

The first mode of compound time, is known by a figure 6 placed over a 4, has six crotchets in a measure, sung in the time of two seconds, two beats in a bar.

The second mode is known by a figure 6 over an 8, has six quavers in a measure sung in the time of one second, two beats in a bar.

In modes of time that are distinguished by figures, it may be observed, that the under figure shows into how many parts the Semibreve is divided, and the upper figure, how many of the same parts fill a bar.

NOTE. In all modes of time, the hand falls at the beginning of a bar, and rises at the end, as the above examples show; the d stands for down, and u for up; and the figures mark the number of beats in each bar.

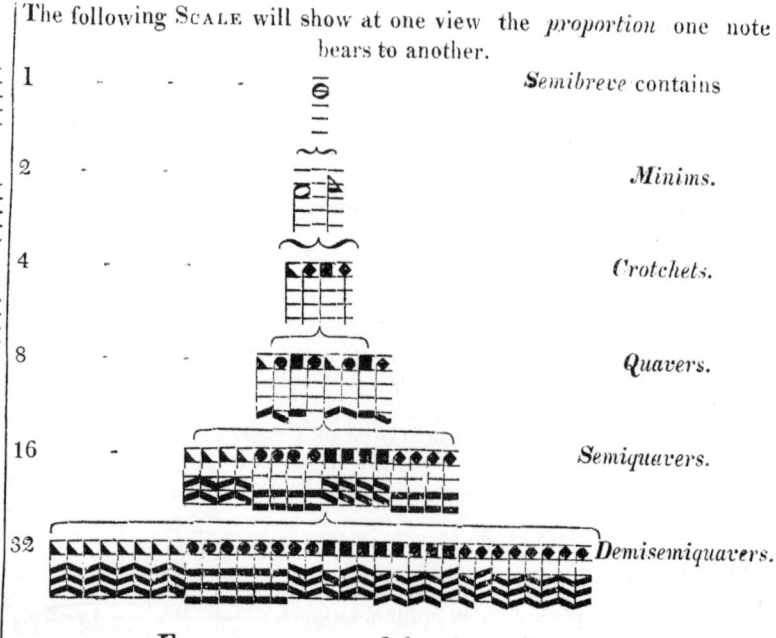

The following SCALE will show at one view the *proportion* one note bears to another.

1 — *Semibreve* contains

2 — *Minims.*

4 — *Crotchets.*

8 — *Quavers.*

16 — *Semiquavers.*

32 — *Demisemiquavers.*

EXPLANATION of the above SCALE.

THIS scale comprehends the six musical notes, with their rests and the proportion they bear to each other.

1. The *Semibreve*, is now the longest note used, it is the measure note, and guideth all the others.

The *Minim,* is but half the length of the semibreve and has a tail to it.

The *Crotchet,* is but half the length of the minim, and has a black head.

The *Quaver,* is but half the length of the crochet, having one turn to its tail, which is crooked, sometimes one way and sometimes another.

The *Semiquaver,* is but half the length of the quaver, having two turns to its tail, which turns are likewise crooked variously.

The *Demisemiquaver,* is half the length of the semiquaver, and has three turns to its tail, also crooked variously.

All Rests signify that you must keep silent so long time as takes to sound the notes they represent, excepting the semibreve rest, which is called the Bar rest, always filling a bar, be the mood of time what it may.

THE RESTS.
Semibreve Minim Crotchet Quaver Semiquaver Demisemiquavers 2 bars 4 bars 8 bars

When there is neither a flat nor a sharp set at the beginning of any tune the Mi will be found, in all parts of music, on that line or space of the stave which is called B :

But if there is one flat, on   E   And if one sharp on   F
if two flats, on   A   if two sharps, on   C
if three flats, on   D   if three sharps on   G
if four flats, on   G   if four sharps, on   D

All the parts of music, sung together, are connected with a 'Brace

Scholars, will easily acquire the knowledge of *faw sol law-ing*, by attending to the following example of the shapes and names of the four notes, viz.

FAW has a triangle.   SOL a round.   LAW a square, and   MI a diamond shape.

GENERAL OBSERVATIONS.

We shall close this introduction, with extracting the following general observations;

ACCENT* is a stress of the voice on a particular part of a measure, which is according to the subdivision of it. The first mode of common time, if divided into eight quavers, has four accents in a measure. The third and fourth mode if divided into four equal parts, has the accent on the first and fourth. The triple time mode, has two accents in a measure, the first is the strongest the second is weak. Compound time when divided into six equal parts, has the accent on the first and fourth.

In beating time which should be done with the hand alone, in performing vocal music, the first mode of common time may be began with the hand going down, resting the end of the fingers on the thing beat upon: the second beat, bring down the heel of the hand without raising the fingers; for the third beat, bring the hand towards the left shoulder; for the fourth, bring it to its first position, the two first beats in triple are performed as the two first in common time; for the third beat raise the hand to its first position.

In tuning the voice, let it be as smooth as possible, neither forcing it through the nose nor blowing it through the teeth, with the mouth shut. Ease and freedom should be particularly observed.

* *From the above I would not have any persons forget that the music should always conform to the words, and if an emphatic word fall on the unaccented part of a bar, the accent should always accompany it.*

A genteel pronunciation is one of the greatest ornaments in Music: Every word should be spoken clear and distinct as possible. It is this, that, in a great measure, gives vocal music the preference to instrumental, by enjoying, at the same time, the sweets of harmony, together with the sense of what is expressed in these harmonious strains.

Several graces such as the trill, turn, &c. are omitted, as of being of no use especially to learners.

The proper proportion of the parts is generally said to be three on the bass, one on the tenor, one on the counter, and two on the treble.

Let the bass be sung bold and majestic, the tenor firm and manly, the counter clear and lofty, and the treble soft and delicate.

High notes should be sung soft, but not faint; low notes full but not harsh.

Notes should not be struck abruptly, like the report of a smith's hammer; but should be begun and ended soft, swelling gently as the air of the tune requires. Notes of two beats admit of a double swell: the first fullest; the second soft, like an echo.

Tunes on a sharp key are expressive of cheerfulness, and suitable for psalms of thanksgiving and praise; Tunes on a flat key are expressive of sorrow, and are suitable to subjects of prayer and penitence. This rule seems to be unnoticed by choristers in general, although it is as inconsistent in nature to sing a cheerful subject to a flat Key, as on the contrary to mourn at thanksgivings, or rejoice at funerals. We give thanks in sound, and mourn in sense, the tune and sentiment being at variance. And the music must be either without impression, or oppose its designed end.—But when music and subject agree, they mutually assist each other, and fill us with ardor, solemnity, and delight, while engaged in the sacred worship of the Deity.

The concluding note should not be broken off abruptly, nor die away faintly, but be sounded smoothly, gently swelling the last beat like an echo, and all conclude at the same instant.

Decency in the position of the body, and beating time are strictly to be adhered to. Likewise a becoming seriousness, while singing sacred words, adds dignity to the performance & renders it at once respectable & solemn.

Musical Terms.

Adagio. Denotes the slowest movement; and is the proper name often first mood in common time.

Allegro. Denotes a quick movement, and is the name of the third mood in common time.

Andante. Implies a moderate, equal and distinct manner of performing.

Affetuoso. Tender and affectionate.

Crescendo. This implies that the force of the voice must increase gradually till the strain is ended.

Diminuendo or *Dim.* Means the reverse of the foregoing, and is sometimes set in opposition to it; when properly performed they make no trifling addition to the beauties of music.

Duetto. Two parts only.

Trio. A tune in three parts.

Dacapo. To conclude with the first strain.

Divoto. In a devout manner.

Forte or *For.* Full, loud or strong.

Fortissimo or *Fortis.* Louder than forte.

Grave. Denotes a slow movement, between Adagio and Largo; it requires also a solemn manner of singing.

Languissiant. In a languishing manner.

Meastoso. Passages which have this term placed over them, must be performed slow, with majesty and grandeur.

Moderato. Somewhat slower than the true time.

Mezza piano. Not so soft as piano.

Piano or *Pia.* Directs the performer to sing soft like an echo.

Pianissimo or *Pianis.* Very soft.

Solo. One part alone.

Vivace. In a lively cheerful manner

Vigoroso. With strength and firmness.

LESSONS FOR TUNING THE VOICE.

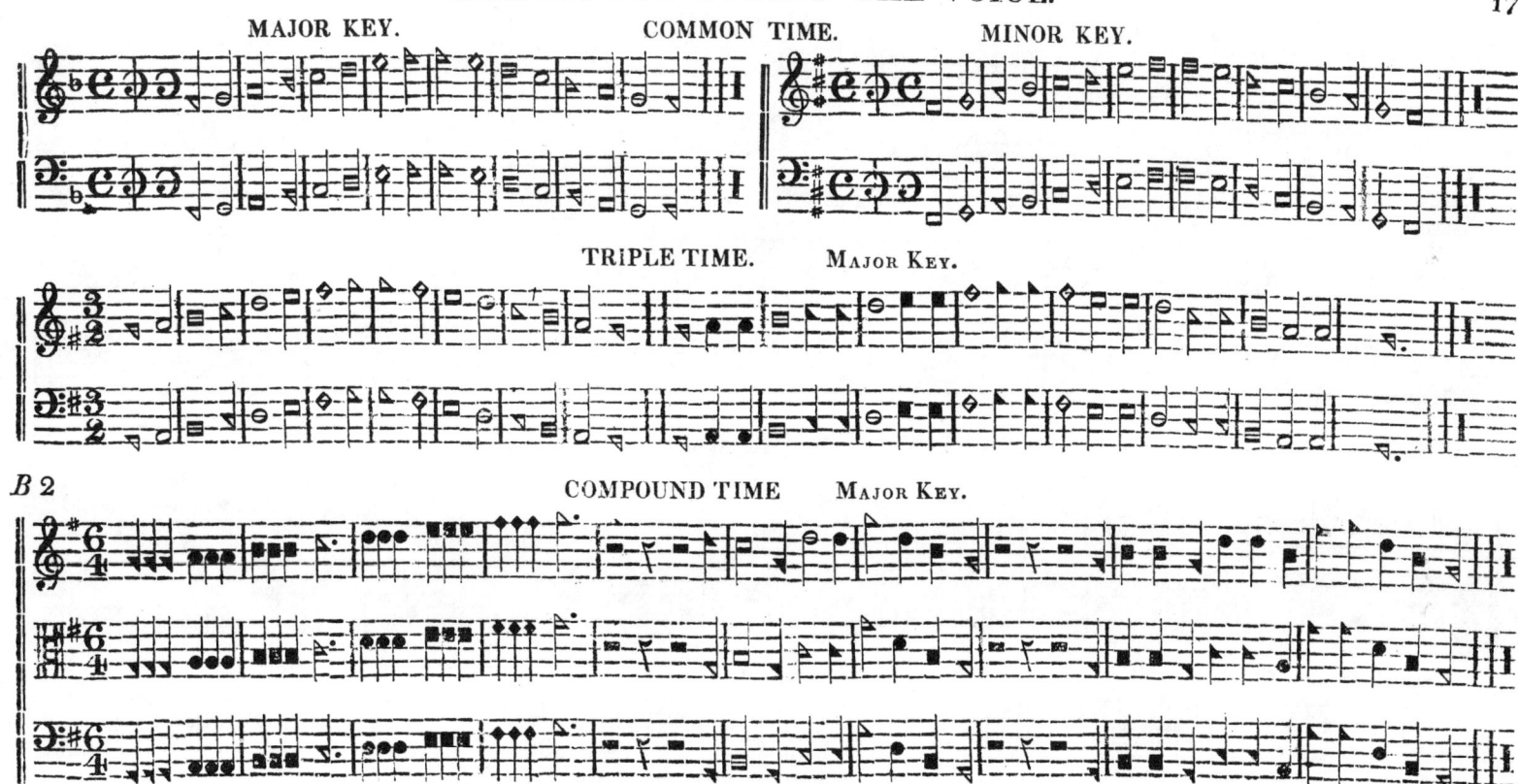

MAJOR KEY. COMMON TIME.   MINOR KEY.

TRIPLE TIME.   Major Key.

COMPOUND TIME   Major Key.

BREWER. L. M. Major Key on F.

Now to the pow'r of God supreme, Be everlasting honors giv'n; He saves from hell, we bless his name, He calls our wandering feet to heav'n.

SHARON. S. M. Major Key on F.

Come, ye that love the Lord, And let our joys be known; Join in a song with sweet accord. Join &c. And thus surround the throne. And thus, &c.

2. The sorrows of the mind, Be banish'd from the place: Religion never was design'd, Religion &c. To make our pleasures less, To make, &c.
3. Let those refuse to sing, That never knew our God, But fav'rites of the heav'nly King, But &c. May speak their joys abroad, May &c.

VERMONT. C. M. Minor Key E.

In vain we lavish out our lives, To gather empty wind, The choicest blessings earth can yield, Will starve an hungry mind.

Come and the Lord shall feed our souls With more substantial meat, With such as saints in glory love, With such as angels eat.

CONSOLATION. C. M. Minor Key on A.

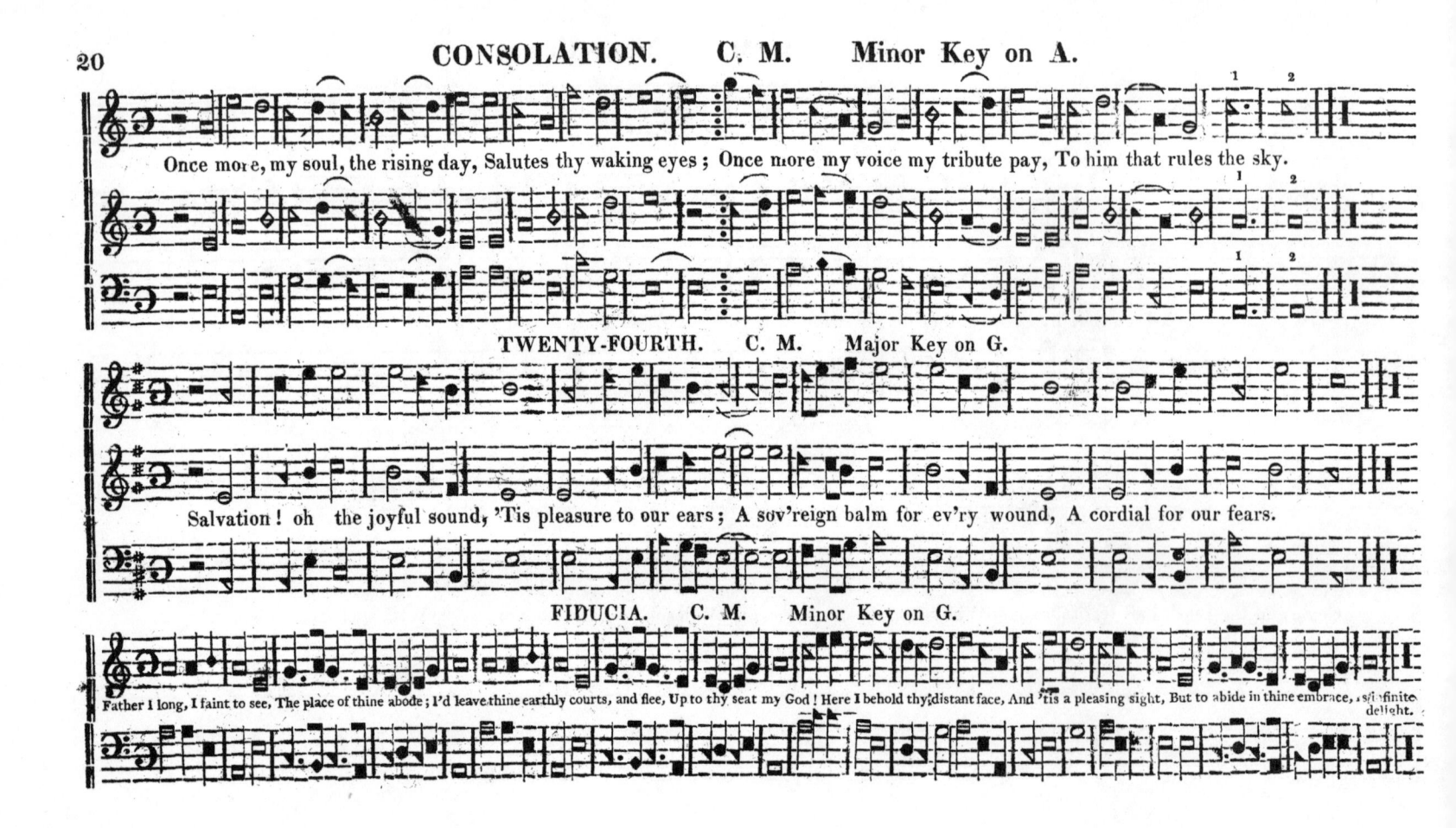

Once more, my soul, the rising day, Salutes thy waking eyes; Once more my voice my tribute pay, To him that rules the sky.

TWENTY-FOURTH. C. M. Major Key on G.

Salvation! oh the joyful sound, 'Tis pleasure to our ears; A sov'reign balm for ev'ry wound, A cordial for our fears.

FIDUCIA. C. M. Minor Key on G.

Father I long, I faint to see, The place of thine abode; I'd leave thine earthly courts, and flee, Up to thy seat my God! Here I behold thy distant face, And 'tis a pleasing sight, But to abide in thine embrace, is infinite delight.

VERNON. L. M. Minor Key on E.

Lord what a heav'n of saving grace, Shines thro the beauties of thy face; And lights our passion to a flame! Lord, how we love thy charming name!

NINETY-FIFTH. C. M. Major Key on G.

When I can read my title clear, To mansions in the skies, I bid farewell to ev'ry fear, to ev'ry fear, And wipe my weeping eyes.

I bid   I bid

MOUNT ZION. S. M. Major Key on C.

The hill of Zion yields a thousand sacred sweets, Before we reach the heav'nly road, Or walk the golden streets, Then let our songs abound, And ev'ry tear be dry,

Then let our songs abound, And ev'ry tear be dry; We're marching thro

Then let our songs abound, And ev'ry tear be dry; We're marching thro Immanuel's ground

Were marching thro Immanuel's ground, To fairer worlds on high. We're &c. We're march - - - ing thro, We're marching thro Immanuels ground, To fairer worlds on high.

Immanuel's ground, To fairer worlds on high We're marching thro, We're marching thro, We're marching thro, We're marching thro, We're marching thro Immanuel's ground To fairer worlds on high.

To fairer worlds on high. We're marching thro, We're marching thro, We're marching thro, We're marching, marching thro Immanuel's ground, We're marching thro Immanuel's ground, To &c.

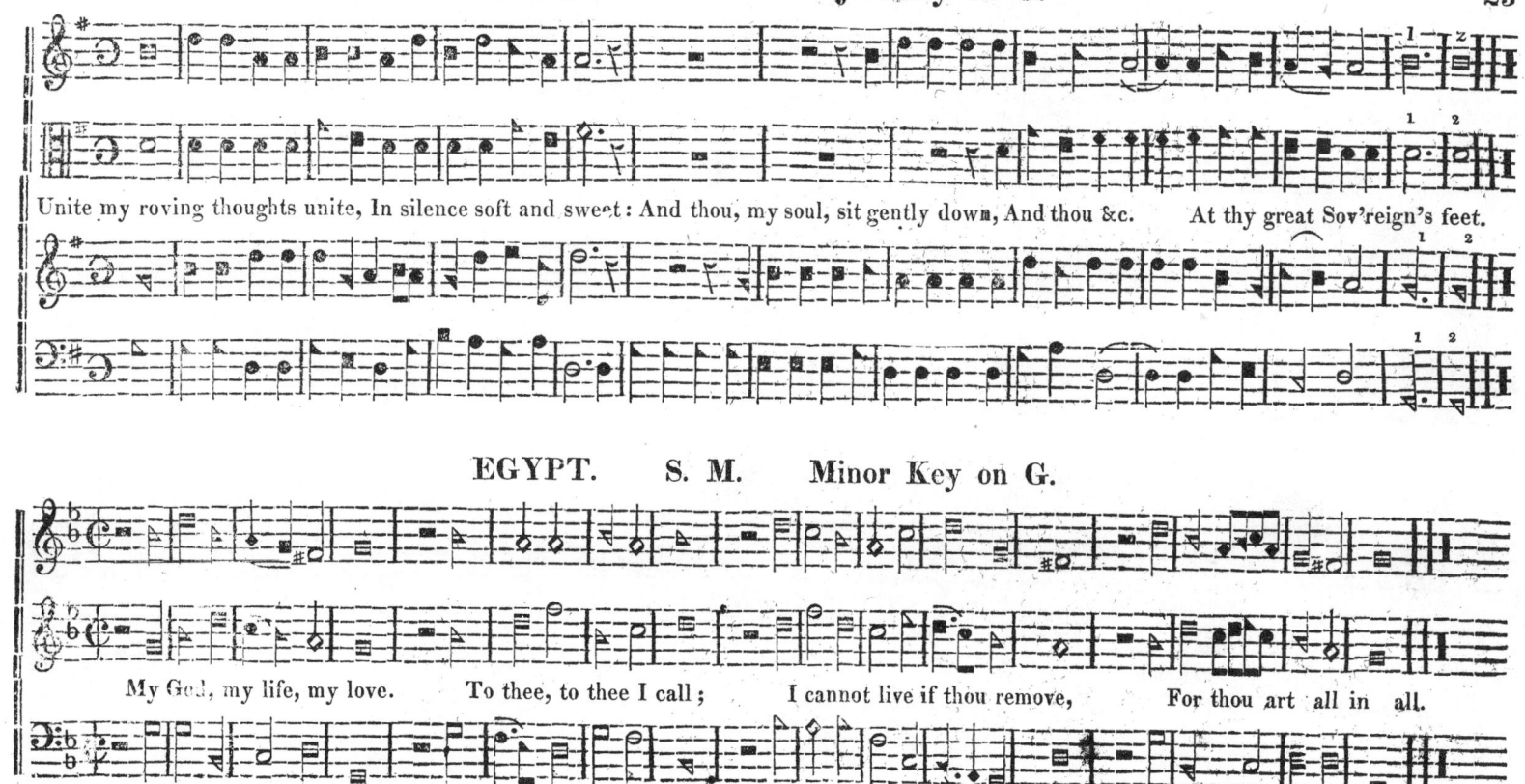

CANAAN. G. M. Major Key on G.

Unite my roving thoughts unite, In silence soft and sweet: And thou, my soul, sit gently down, And thou &c.   At thy great Sov'reign's feet.

EGYPT. S. M. Minor Key on G.

My God, my life, my love.   To thee, to thee I call;   I cannot live if thou remove,   For thou art all in all.

NINETY-THIRD.   S. M.   Major Key on C.

Raise your triumphant songs, To an immortal tune, Let the whole earth resound the deeds Celestial grace hath done.

MOUNT-PLEASAT.   C. M.   Major Key on A.

Pia.   *Forte.*

My God the spring of all my joys, The life of my delights; The glory of my brightest days, And comfort of my nights.   And comfort &c.

TRUMPET. L. M. Major Key on G.

He comes! he comes! the trumpets sound, And loudly rends the vast profound; Earth, sea and skies astonish'd shake. To judgment come—ye dead awake. Halle - lu - jah, Halle - lu - jah,

Continued.

Halle - lu - jah. Praise the Lord.

2. Behold, behold, what myriads rise!
   See! see what glory fills the skies!
   The dreadful volumes open shine;
   O! mercy, Lord; for mercy's thine. Hallelujah.
3. The hour, the awful hour is come,
   Fix'd, ever fix'd is human doom,
   The earth dissolves, heav'n melts away;
   O! shield me, Savior, in that day. Hallelujah.

ISLE OF WHITE. C. M. Minor Key on A.

Lord, shall we part with gold for dross, With solid good for show? Outlive our bliss, and mourn our loss, In ev - er - lasting wo!

MERTON. 6's & 9. Major Key on D.

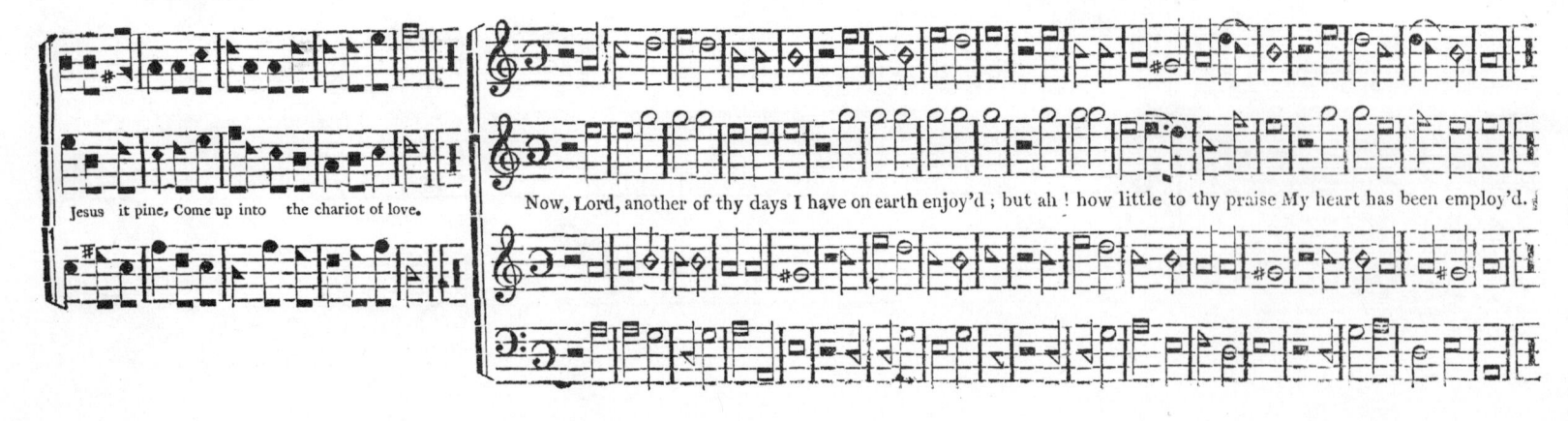

Come let us ascend, My companion and friend, To a taste of the banquet above! If thy heart be as mine, If for Jesus it pine, Come up into the chariot of love. If thy heart be as mine, If for

2 Who in Jesus confide, We are bold to out-ride The storms of affliction beneath! With the prophet we soar To the heavenly shore, And outfly all the arrows of death.
3 By faith we are come To our permanent home, By hope we the rapture improve: By love we still rise, And look down on the skies, For the heaven of heavens is love.
4 Who on earth can conceive, How happy we live In the palace of God the great King! What a concert of praise, When our Jesus's grace The whole heavenly company sing.
5 What a rapturous song, When the glorified throng In the spirit of harmony join: Join all the glad choirs, Hearts, voices and lyres, And the burden is mercy divine.
6 Hallelujah, the cry, To the king of the sky, To the great everlasting I AM; To the Lamb that was slain, And liveth again, Hallelujah to God and the Lamb.

Continued.

Jesus it pine, Come up into the chariot of love.

WINDSOR. C. M. Minor Key on A.

Now, Lord, another of thy days I have on earth enjoy'd; but ah! how little to thy praise My heart has been employ'd.

GOSPEL TRUMPET. 8's & 4.

Hark! how the gospel trumpet sounds, Thro' all the earth the echo bounds; And Jesus by redeeming blood, Is bringing sinners back to God, And guides them safely by his word, To endless day.

2 Hail! all victor'ous conq'ring Lord! Be thou by all thy works adored, Who undertook for sinful man, And brought salvation through thy name. That we with thee may ever reign In endless day.
3 Fight on, ye conq'ring souls, fight on, And when the conquest you have won, The palm of victory you shall bear, And in his kingdom have a share, And crowns of glory ever wear In endless day.
4 There we shall in sweet chorus join, And saints and angels all combine, To sing of his redeeming love, When rolling years shall cease to move; and this shall be our theme above In endless day.

WATERFORD. 6's & 8.   MAJOR Key on C.

Counter.

How pleas'd & bless'd was I, To hear the people cry, 'Come let us seek our God to day; Yes, with a cheerful zeal, We'll haste to Zion's hill, And there our vows & honors pay.'

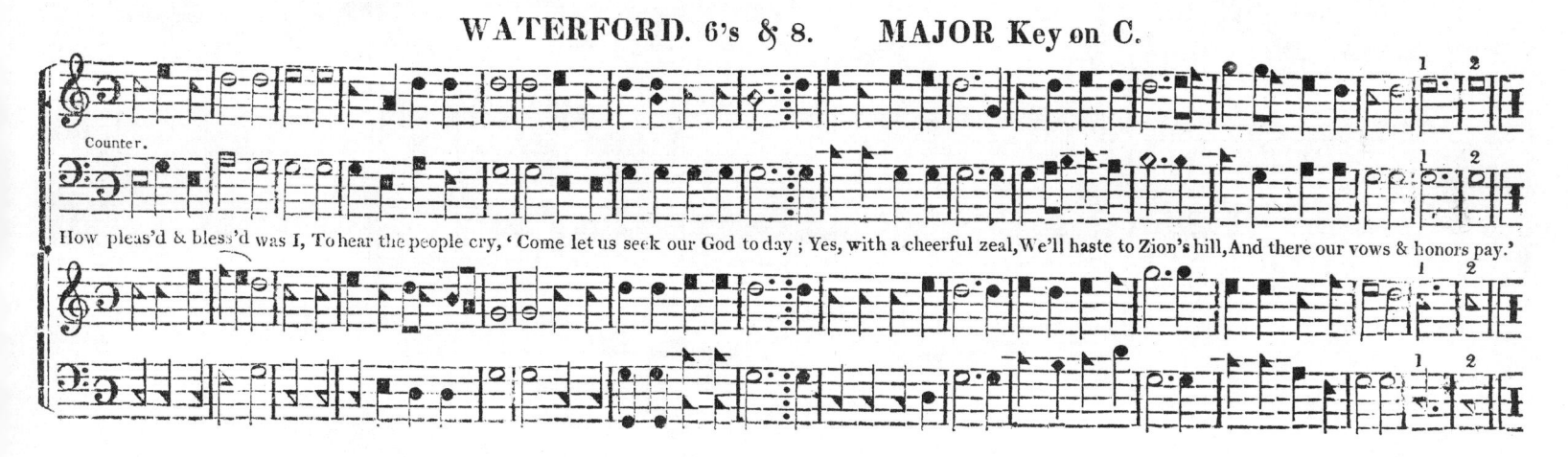

DAWNING LIGHT. 10's. Major Key on B.

In boundless mercy, gracious Lord appear; Darkness dispel—the humble mourner cheer; the humble mourner cheer. Vain thoughts remove, Vain &c. Melt down this flinty heart, Cause ev'ry soul, Cause

Continued.

ev'ry soul To choose the better part.

TWENTY-FIFTH. S. M. Minor Key on A.

I lift my soul to God; My trust is in his name, Let not my foes that seek my blood, still triumph in my shame, Still &c.

PLYMOUTH-DOCK. L. P. M. Major Key on G.

Jesus how precious is thy name! The great Jehovah's darling Thou! O let me catch th' immortal flame, With which angelic bosoms glow! Since angels love thee, I would love, And imi-

2. My *Prophet* thou, my heavenly guide, Thy sweet instructions I will hear; The words that from thy lips proceed, O how divinely sweet they are! Thee my great *Prophet* I would love, And imitate the bless'd above.
3. My great *High Priest*, whose precious blood Did once atone upon the cross: Who now doth intercede with God, And plead the friendless sinners cause; In thee I trust; Thee would I love, And imitate the bless'd above.
4. My *King* supreme, to thee I bow, A willing subject at thy feet; All other lords I disavow, and to thy government submit, My *Saviour King*, this heart would love, And imitate the bless'd above.

C 2. Continued.

tate the bless'd above.

SHIELDS. 8 & 7. Major Key on A.

Come Thou fount of every blessing, Tune my heart to sing thy grace;
Streams of mercy never ceasing, Call for songs of loudest praise.
Praise the mount, I'm fixt upon it. Mount of thy redeeming love. Teach me some melodious sonnet, Sung by flaming tongues above;

Da Capo.

2. Here I'll raise mine Ebenezer, Hither by thy help I'm come; And I hope, by thy good pleasure, Safely to arrive at home: Jesus sought me when a stranger, Wand'ring from the fold of God; He to rescue me from danger, Interpos'd his precious blood.
3. O! to grace how great a debtor, Daily I'm constrain'd to be! Let that grace, Lord, like a fetter, Bind my wand'ring heart to thee! Prone to wander, Lord, I feel it; Prone to leave the God I love. Here's my heart, Lord take and seal it, Seal in thy courts above.

HARMONY. 10's & 11's. Major Key on B.

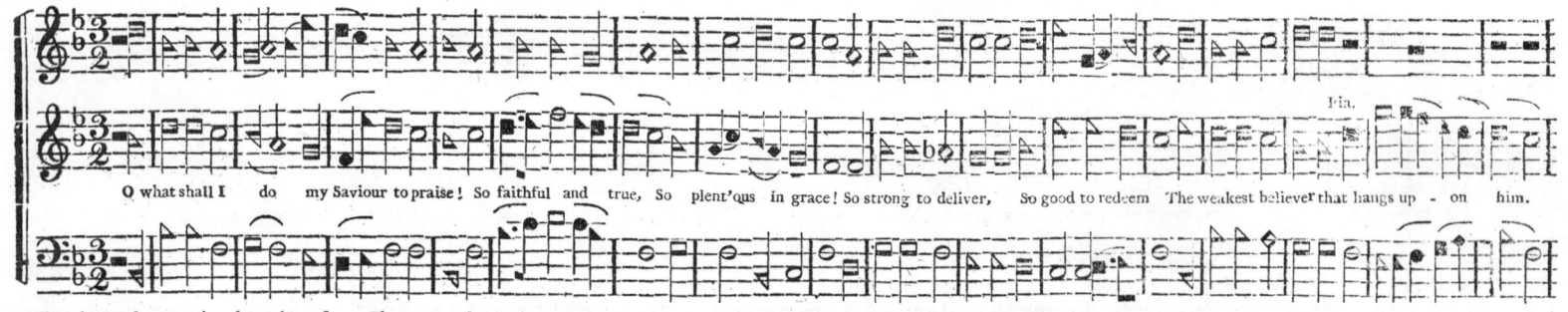

O what shall I do my Saviour to praise! So faithful and true, So plent'ous in grace! So strong to deliver, So good to redeem The weakest believer that hangs up - on him.

2. How happy the man whose heart is set free, The people who can be joyful in thee; Their joy is to walk in the light of thy face, And still they are talking of Jesus's grace.
3. Their daily delight shall be in thy name, They shall as their right thy right'ousness claim; Thy righteousness wearing and cleans'd by thy blood. Bold shall they appear in the presence of God.
4. For thou art their boast, their glory and pow'r. And I also trust to see the glad hour, My soul's new creation, a life from the dead- The day of salvation that lifts up my head.
5. For Jesus my Lord is now my defence; I trust in his word, none plucks me from thence, Since I have found favor he all things will do; My King and my Saviour shall make me anew.
6. Yes Lord I shall see the bliss of thine own; The secret to me shall soon be made known; For sorrow and sadness I joy shall receive And share in the gladness of all that believe.

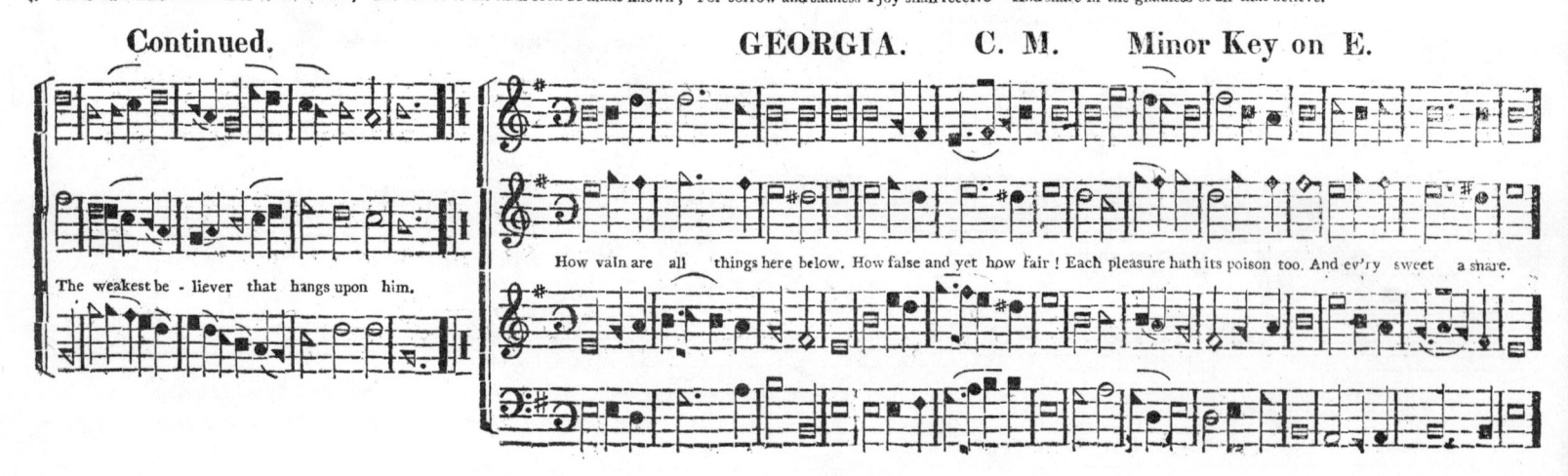

Continued.

The weakest be-liever that hangs upon him.

GEORGIA. C. M. Minor Key on E.

How vain are all things here below. How false and yet how fair! Each pleasure hath its poison too. And ev'ry sweet a snare.

NATIVITY. C. M. Major Key on G.

Come let us lift our joyful eyes, Up to the courts above, And smile to see our Father there, Up - on a throne of love. Up - on a throne of love.

WILLIAMSTOWN. L. M. Minor Key on G.

Shew pity, Lord; O Lord forgive; Let a repenting rebel live; Are not thy mercies large and free? May not a sinner trust in thee?

HAMILTON. L. M. Major Key on C.

God is the refuge of his saints, When storms of sharp distress invade; Ere we can offer our complaints, Behold him present with his aid.

Continued.

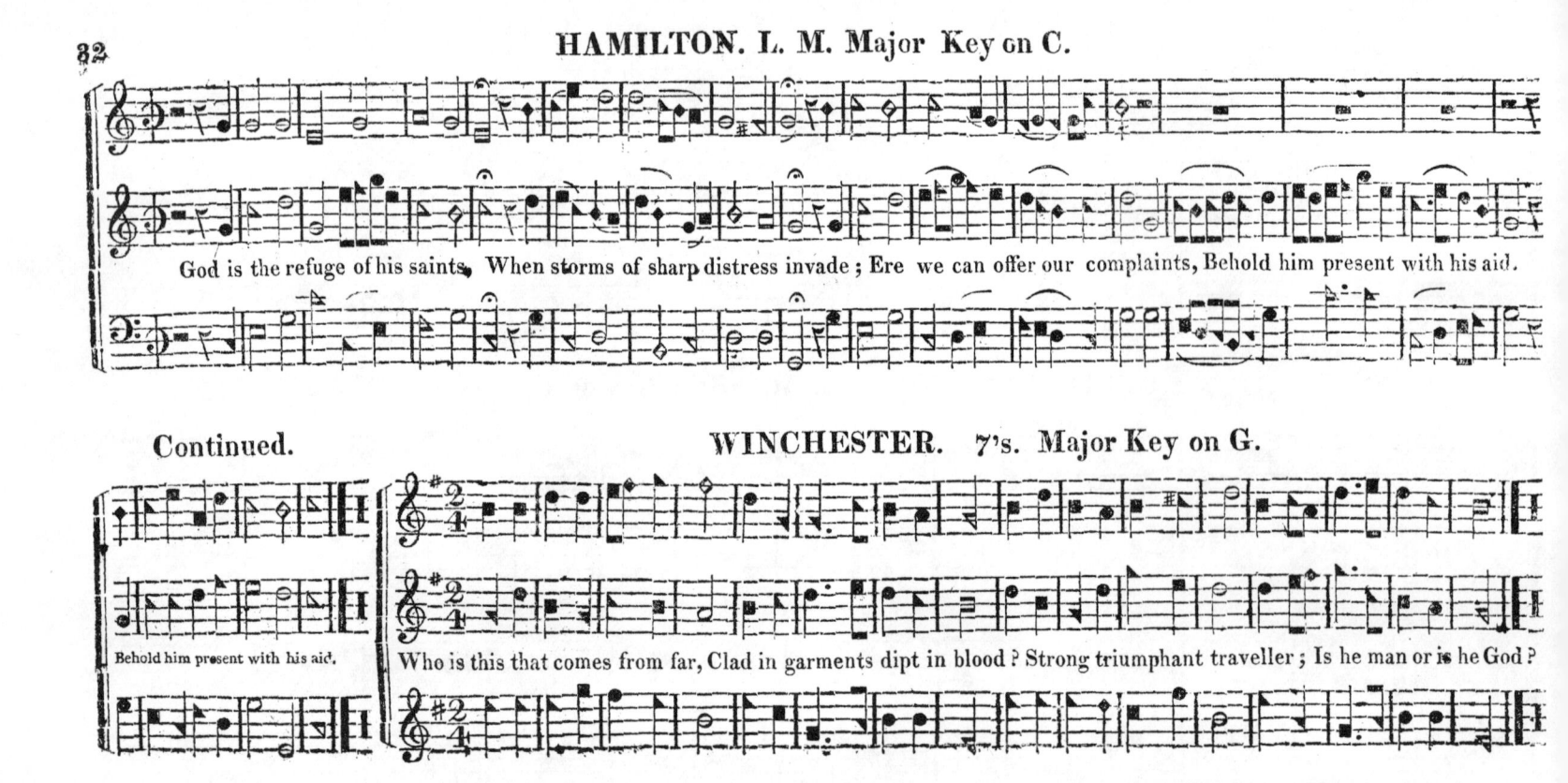

Behold him present with his aid.

WINCHESTER. 7's. Major Key on G.

Who is this that comes from far, Clad in garments dipt in blood? Strong triumphant traveller; Is he man or is he God?

ST. JOHNS. 8. 8. 6. Major Key on A.

Begin, my soul, th' exalted lay, Let each enraptur'd thought obey, And praise th' almighty name. Lo! heav'n, and earth, and seas and skies, In one me - lo - dious concert rise, To swell th' inspiring theme. To swell &c.

SCHENECTADY. L. M. Major Key on E.

From all who dwell below the skies, Let the Creator's praise arise, Let the Redeemer's name be sung, Thro' ev'ry land, by ev'ry tongue. Eternal are thy mercies, Lord, Eternal are thy mercies, Lord, Eternal truth attends thy word; Thy praise shall sound from shore to shore; Thy praise &c. Till suns shall set and rise no more.

BOSTON. C. M. Major Key on B.

Methinks I see a heav'nly hosts Of angels on the wing; Methinks I hear their cheerful notes, So merrily they sing.

Let all your fears be banish'd hence; Glad tidings we proclaim, For there's a Savior born to day, And Jesus is his name.

PHŒBUS. C. M. Minor Key on F.

Lord, in the morning thou shalt hear, My voice ascending high, To thee will I direct my prayer, To thee lift up mine eye. Up to the hills where Christ is gone, To plead for all his saints, Presenting at his Father's throne, Presenting at his Father's throne, Our songs and our complaints.

Our so — — — ngs &c.

Presenting &c.

GOSPEL TRUMP. Major Key on G. 37

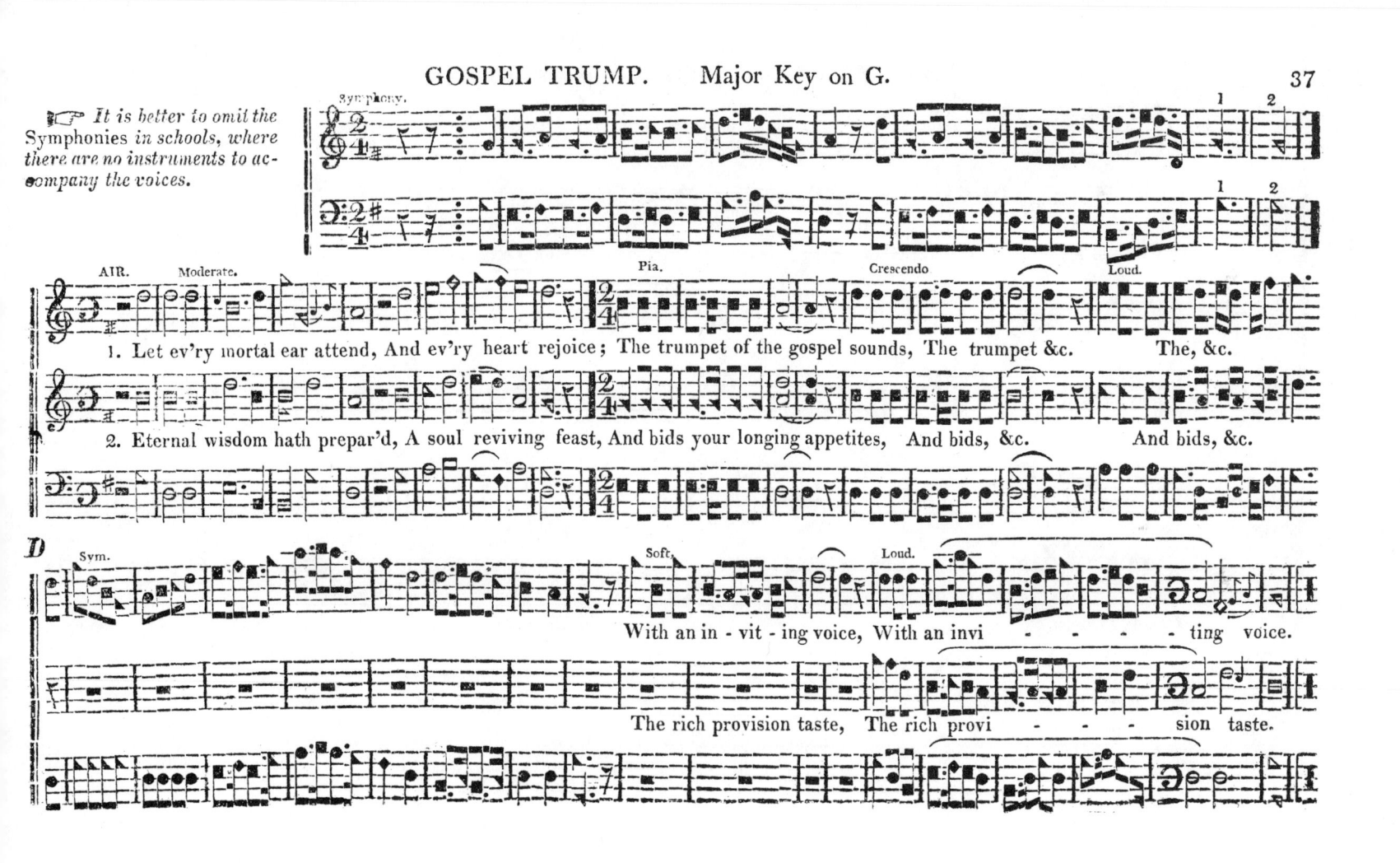

☞ *It is better to omit the Symphonies in schools, where there are no instruments to accompany the voices.*

1. Let ev'ry mortal ear attend, And ev'ry heart rejoice; The trumpet of the gospel sounds, The trumpet &c.   The, &c.

2. Eternal wisdom hath prepar'd, A soul reviving feast, And bids your longing appetites,   And bids, &c.   And bids, &c.

With an in - vit - ing voice, With an invi - - - ting voice.

The rich provision taste, The rich provi - - - sion taste.

BELLEVUE. P. M. Major Key on F.

Ye tribes of Adam join, With heav'n & earth & seas, And offer notes divine To your Creator's praise.

Ye holy, &c.

Ye holy throng of angels bright, In holy throng, &c.

Ye holy throng, &c. Ye Ye holy throng of angels bright, In worlds of light Begin the song.

Ye

worlds of light, Begin the song. Ye

BABYLONIAN CAPTIVITY. P. M. Minor Key on F.

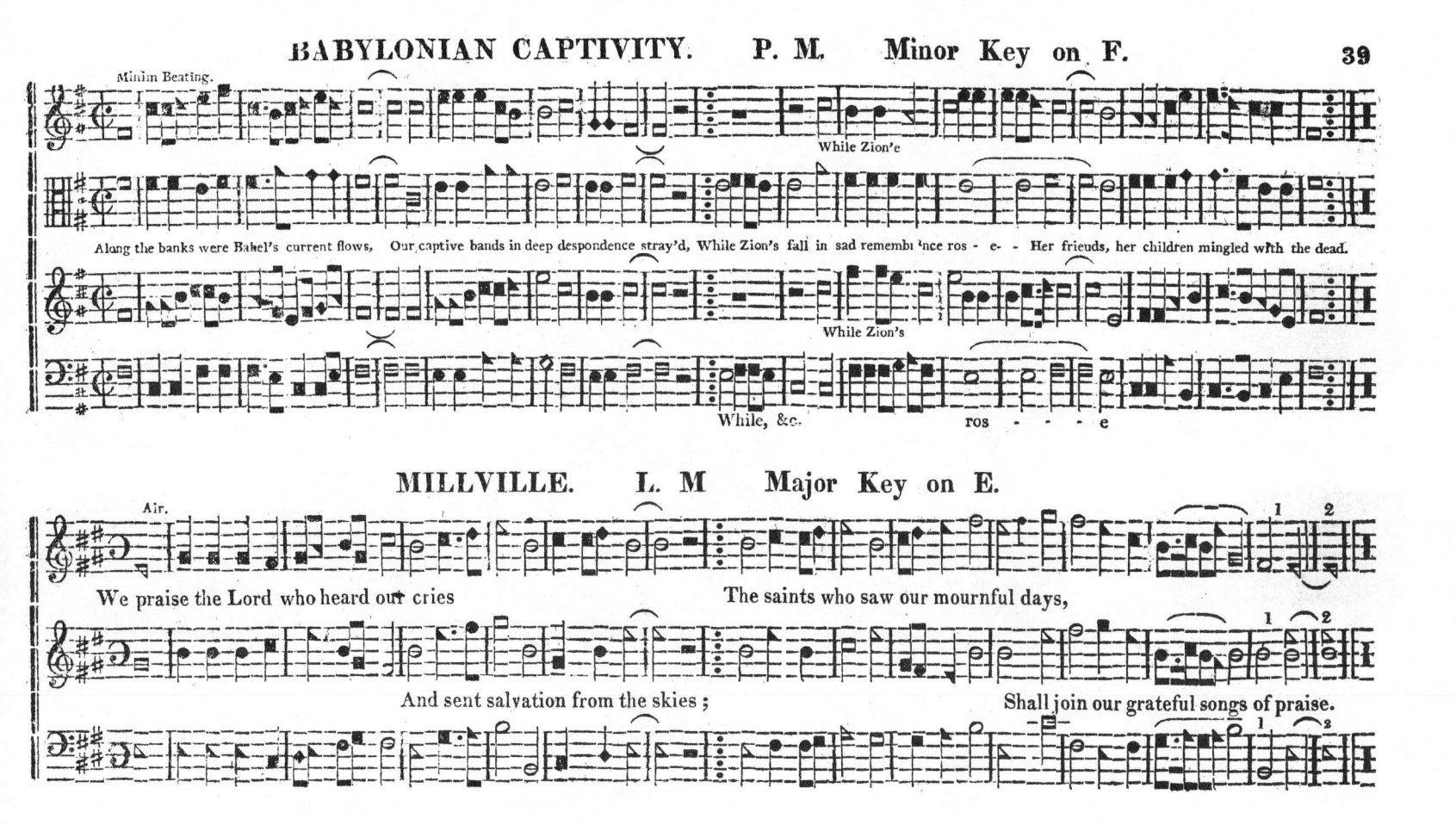

Along the banks were Babel's current flows, Our captive bands in deep despondence stray'd, While Zion's fall in sad remembrance ros- e- - Her friends, her children mingled with the dead.

While Zion's

While, &c. ros - - - e

MILLVILLE. L. M Major Key on E.

We praise the Lord who heard our cries The saints who saw our mournful days,

And sent salvation from the skies; Shall join our grateful songs of praise.

FORSTER. C. M. Minor Key on E.

Ye weary heavy laden souls, Who are oppressed sore; Ye trav'lers thro' the wilderness, To Canaan's peaceful shore;

Thro' chilling winds and beating rains, The waters deep and cold, And enemies surrounding you Take courage and be bold.

Tho' storms and hurricanes arise,
  The desert all around,
And fi'ry serpents oft appear,
  Thro' the enchanting ground;
Dark nights, and clouds, and gloomy fear,
  And dragons often roar,
But while the gospel trump we hear,
  We'll press for Canaan's shore.

We're often like the lonesome dove,
  Who mourns her absent mate,
From hill to hill, from vale to vale,
  Her sorrows to relate,
But Canaan's land is just before,
  Sweet spring is coming on
A few more winds and beating rain
  And winter will be gone.

Sometimes like mountains to the sky,
  Black Jordan's billows roar;
Which often make the pilgrims fear
  They never will get o'er,
But let us gain Mount Pisgah's top,
  And view the vernal plain,
To fright our soul may Jordan roar,
  And hell may rage in vain.

Methinks I now begin to see
  The borders of that land,
The trees of life with heav'nly fruit
  In beauteous order stand;
The wint'ry time is past and gone,
  Sweet flowers do appear,
The fiftieth year is now roll'd round,
  The great Sabbatic year.

O! what a glorious sight appears
  To my believing eyes,
Methinks I see Jerusalem,
  A city in the skies!
Bright angels whisp'ring me away,
  O! come, my brother, come;
And I am willing to be gone
  To my eternal home.

By faith I see my gracious God,
  On his eternal throne;
At his right hand the loving Lamb,
  The Spirit Three in One,
O that my faith was strong to rise
  And bear my soul away,
I'd shout salvation to the Lamb,
  In one eternal day.

Farewell, my brethren in the Lord,
  Who are to Canaan bound;
And should we never meet again,
  Till Jubal's trump shall sound,
I hope that I shall meet you there,
  On that delightful shore,
In oceans of delightful bliss
  Where parting is no more.

PILGRIM's FAREWELL. Major Key on G.

Farewell, Farewell, Farewell, my friends, I must be gone. I have no home nor stay with you; I'll take my staff and travel on, Till I a better world can view.

I'll march to Canaan's land I'll land on Canaan's shore, Where pleasures never end, And troubles come no more. Farewell! Farewell! Farewell! my loving friends, farewell.

Farewell, &c. &c. my friends, time rolls along,
Nor waits for mortal cares or bliss;
I'll leave you here and travel on,
Till I arrive were Jesus is.
   I'll march. &c.
Farewell &c.

Farewell, &c. &c. dear brethren in the Lord,
To you I'm bound with cords of love:
But we believe his gracious word,
We all e're long shall meet above.
   I'll march &c.
Farewell &c.

Farewell, &c. &c. ye blooming sons of God,
Sore conflicts yet remain for you;
But dauntless keep the heavenly road
Till Canaan's happy land you view.
   I'll march &c.
Farewell, farewell, farewell, my loving, &c.

D 2

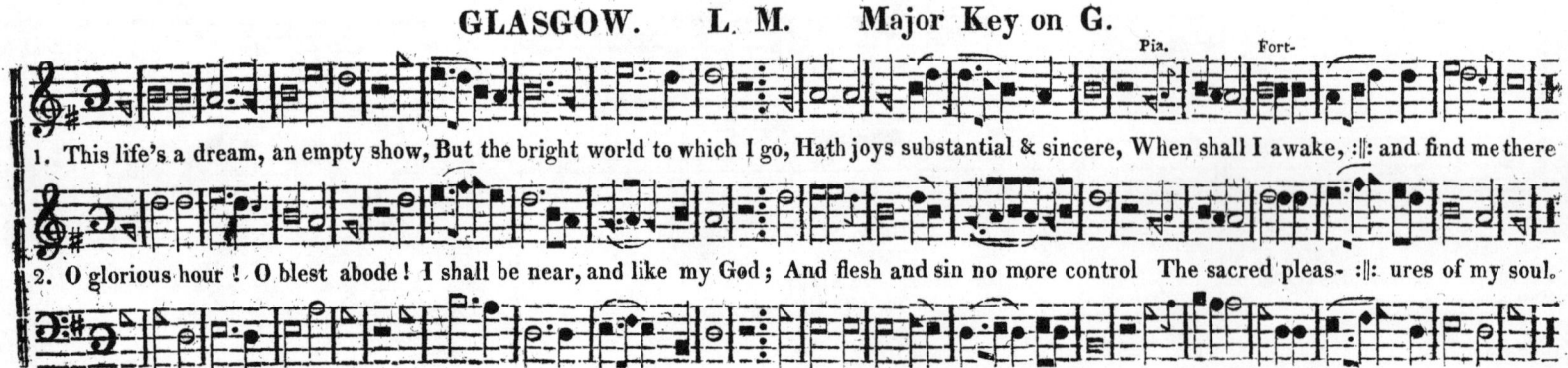

FAIRTON. C. M. Minor Key on A.

O God of mercy hear my call, My load of guilt remove; Break down this separating wall, That bars me from :‖: thy love.

GLASGOW. L. M. Major Key on G.

1. This life's a dream, an empty show, But the bright world to which I go, Hath joys substantial & sincere, When shall I awake, :‖: and find me there

2. O glorious hour! O blest abode! I shall be near, and like my God; And flesh and sin no more control The sacred pleas- :‖: ures of my soul.

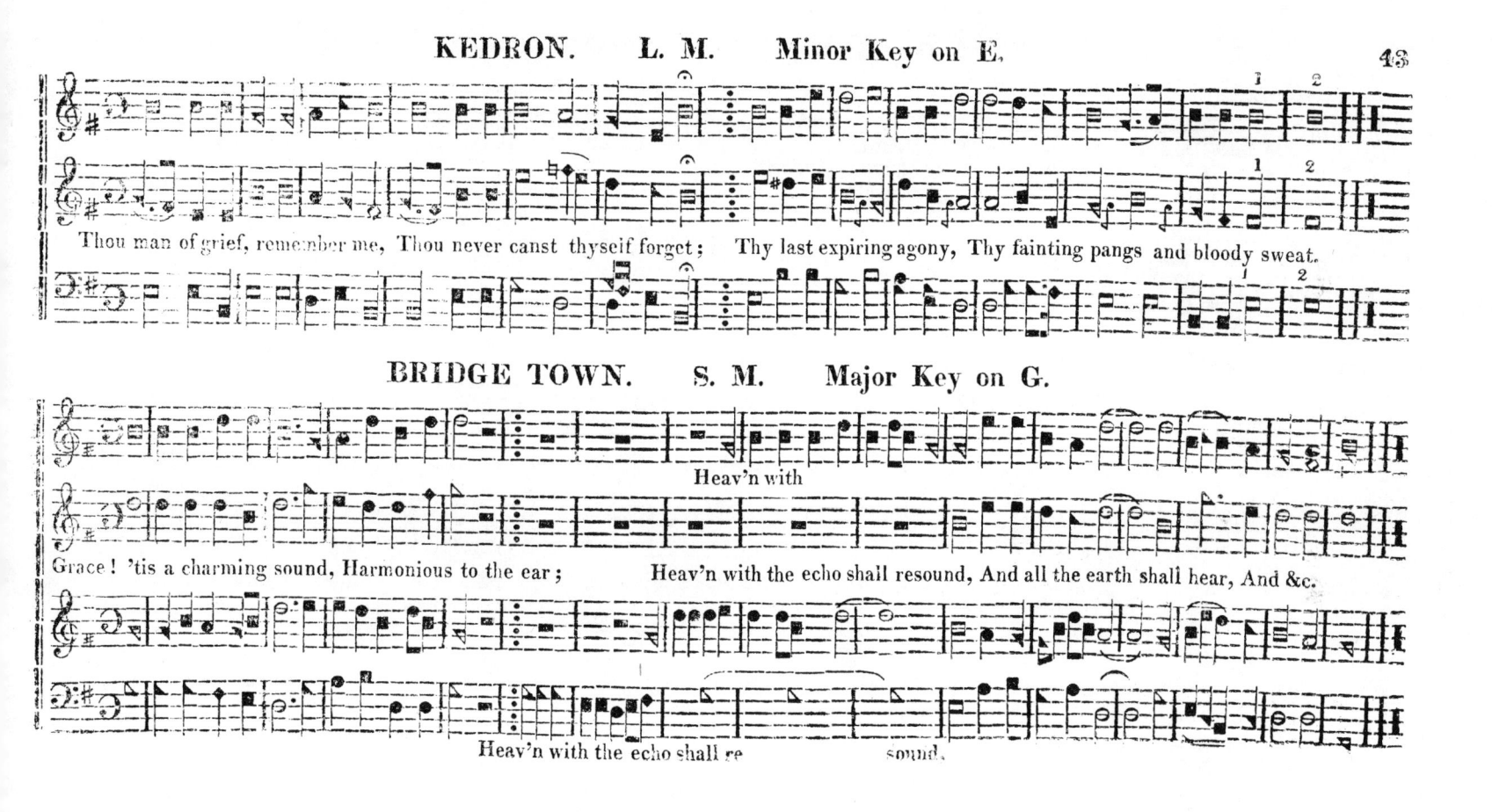

KEDRON. L. M. Minor Key on E.

Thou man of grief, remember me, Thou never canst thyself forget; Thy last expiring agony, Thy fainting pangs and bloody sweat.

BRIDGE TOWN. S. M. Major Key on G.

Grace! 'tis a charming sound, Harmonious to the ear; Heav'n with the echo shall resound, And all the earth shall hear, And &c.

Heav'n with the echo shall re sound.

FALL OF BABYLON. Major Key on G.

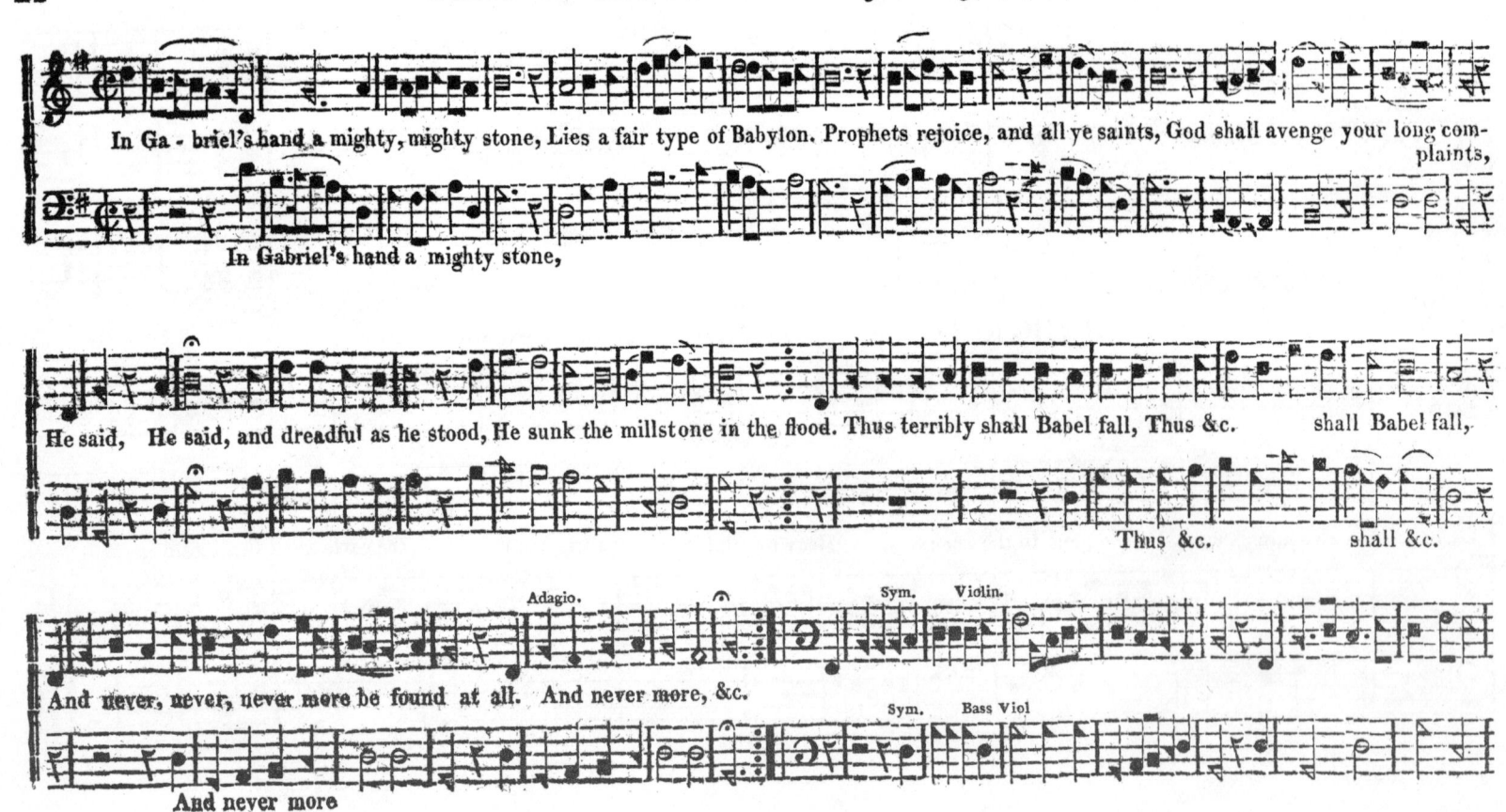

In Ga-briel's hand a mighty, mighty stone, Lies a fair type of Babylon. Prophets rejoice, and all ye saints, God shall avenge your long com-plaints,

In Gabriel's hand a mighty stone,

He said, He said, and dreadful as he stood, He sunk the millstone in the flood. Thus terribly shall Babel fall, Thus &c. shall Babel fall,

Thus &c. shall &c.

Adagio. Sym. Violin.

And never, never, never more be found at all. And never more, &c.

Sym. Bass Viol

And never more

Fall of Babylon, continued.

Haste happy day, :||: :||: That time I long to see,

When ev'ry son of Adam shall be free: Then shall the happy world aloud proclaim, The pleasing wonders, The &c. The pleasing wonders of the Savior's name.

Then shall the happy world aloud proclaim, The pleasing wonders, The &c.

ROAD's-TOWN, P. M. Minor Key on A.

Cheerful. *Slow.*

Blessed are the sons of God, They are bo't with Jesus' blood; They are ransom'd from the grave, Life eternal they shall have; With them number'd may I be, Now and thro' eternity.

With them number'd may I be, With &c.

MOUNT HOPE. A Duet. Major KEY on F. Words by T. Odiorne.

Hark! hark, a Savior's voice, Mountains & hills rebound, Let guilty man rejoice, Let, &c. Woods, rocks & vallies echo back the sound Woods &c. echo back the sound. Behold! a God from heav'n descends, Behold, &c. A clement God kind aud'ance lends—Pities the plaint of wo—Subdues th' infernal foe; Then drops a tear on human crimes, Then &c. And makes man heir to happier, happier climes, And makes, &c.

DISMISSION. P. M. Minor Key on D.

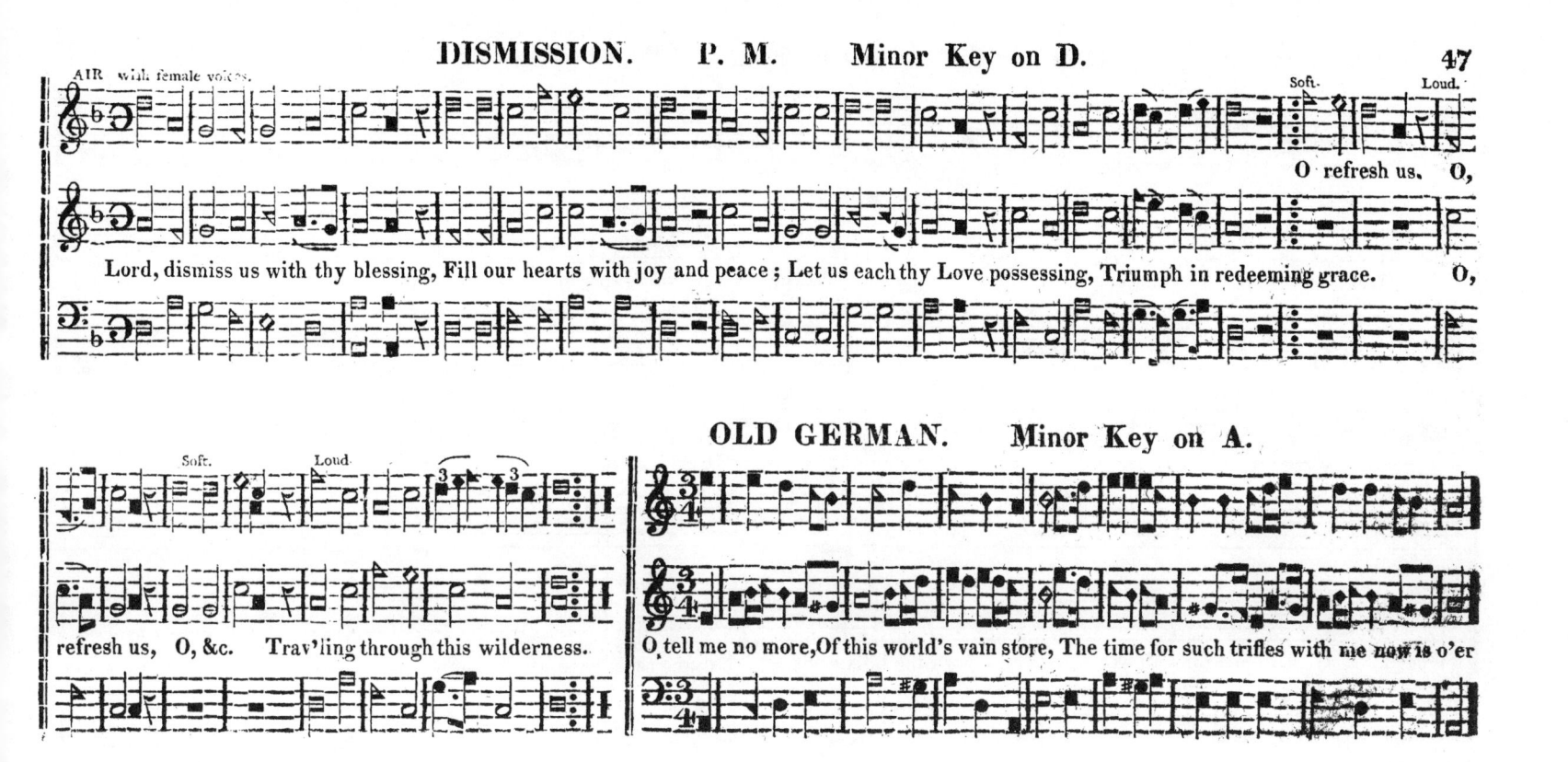

Lord, dismiss us with thy blessing, Fill our hearts with joy and peace; Let us each thy Love possessing, Triumph in redeeming grace. O, O refresh us. O, refresh us, O, &c. Trav'ling through this wilderness.

OLD GERMAN. Minor Key on A.

O, tell me no more, Of this world's vain store, The time for such trifles with me now is o'er

REDEMPTION ANTHEM. Major Key on G.

Hark! hark, glad tidings charm our ears, Angelic mu-sic fills the spheres, Earth spreads the sound with distant mirth, A God, A God is born on earth, A God is born the vallies cry, A God is born the hills reply; Ev'ning repeats to wond'ring morn, A God, A God on earth is born.

Redemption Anthem, continued.

Our frailties long he deign'd to share, The heir of heav'n of pain the heir; By miracles his power he try'd, Preach'd, fasted, sigh'd, groan'd & dy'd.

He liv'd that men might live in peace, He dy'd that death & sin might cease, He rose to prove to hell's fierce pow'rs, Blest immortality is ours.

Redemption Anthem, continued.

Our country love, Our country love, our God adore, Till &c.

O may we strive like him to live, our friends esteem, our foes forgive, Our country love, our God adore Till death and sin shall reign no more.

Our country love, Our country love our God adore.

Our God adore, Till, &c.

MISSIONARY. C. M. Sharp Key on B.

When I can read my title clear To mansions in the skies, I bid farewell to ev'ry fear, I bid &c. I bid &c. And wipe my weeping eyes.

MADISON. L. M. Minor Key on A. 51

Great Shepherd of thine Is-ra-el, Who didst between the cherubs dwell, And led the tribes, thy chosen sheep, Safe thro' the desert and the deep.

Thy church is in the desert now, Shine from on high, and guide us thro' Turn us to thee, thy love restore, We shall be sav'd, and sigh no more.

Thy church

desert now, Shine from on high and guide us thro'

WILMINGTON. P. M. Major Key on G. 4 verses.

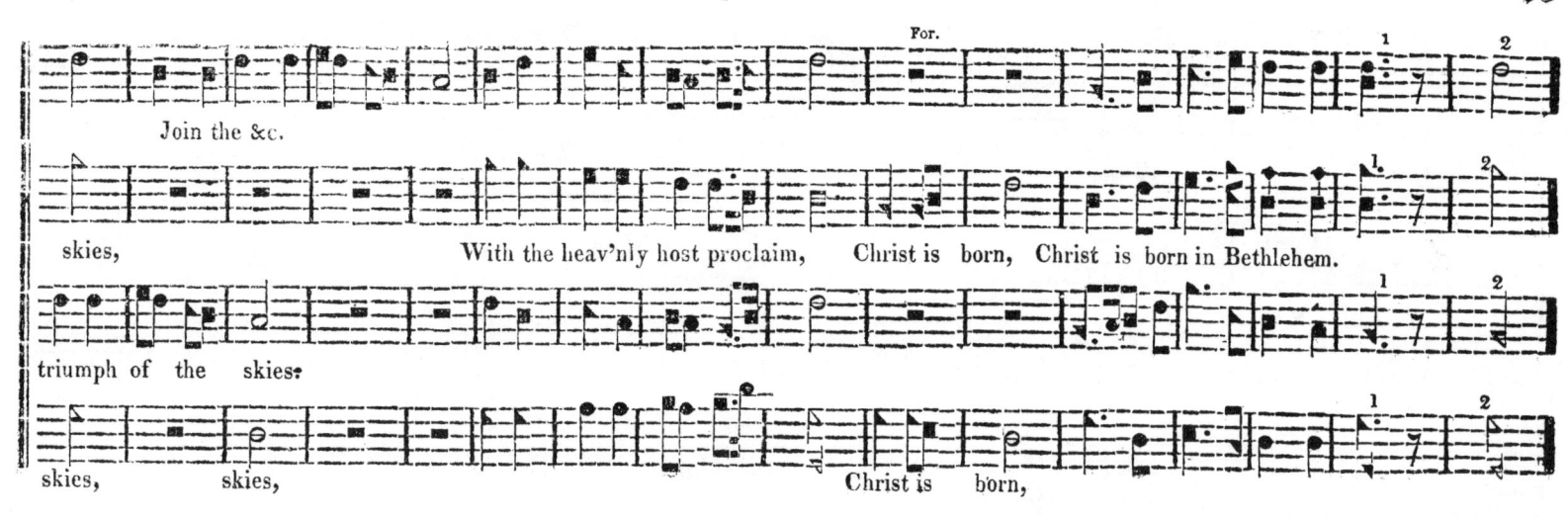

Wilmington, Continued.

53

Join the &c. skies, With the heav'nly host proclaim, Christ is born, Christ is born in Bethlehem.

triumph of the skies; skies, skies, Christ is born,

E 2

Air. Pia. mod.

Christ, by highest heav'n ador'd, Christ, the everlasting Lord; Lowly lays his glories by, Born for men, for men to die.

Wilmington, continued.

Hail! Hail! Hail thou heav'n born Prince of Peace, Hail thou Sun of righteousness, Ris'n with healing in thy wings.

Light and life thy rising brings. Praise ye the Lord. Praise, &c. Praise, &c.

Light and life

life.

EXHORTATION. L. M. Minor Key on A. 55

Now in the heat of youthful blood, Remember your Creator, God; Behold the months come hast'ning on, When you shall say my

joys are gone. When, &c. When &c.

FIDELIA. C. M. Minor Key on A.

Soft and slow.

As on some lonely building top The sparrow tells her moan, Far from the tents of joy and hope, Far, &c.   I set and grieve alone. Sense can afford no real joy To souls that feel thy frown, Lord, 'twas thy hand advanc'd me high; Lord, 'twas &c.   Thy hand hath cast me down. Thy &c.

Thy hand hath cast me down. Lord, &c.

MIDDLE PAXTON. P. M. Major Key on E.

No burning heats by day, Nor blasts of ev'ning air, Shall take my health away, If God be with me there. Thou art my sun, And thou my shade, To guard my head By night or noon.

WOBURN. L. M. Minor Key on A.

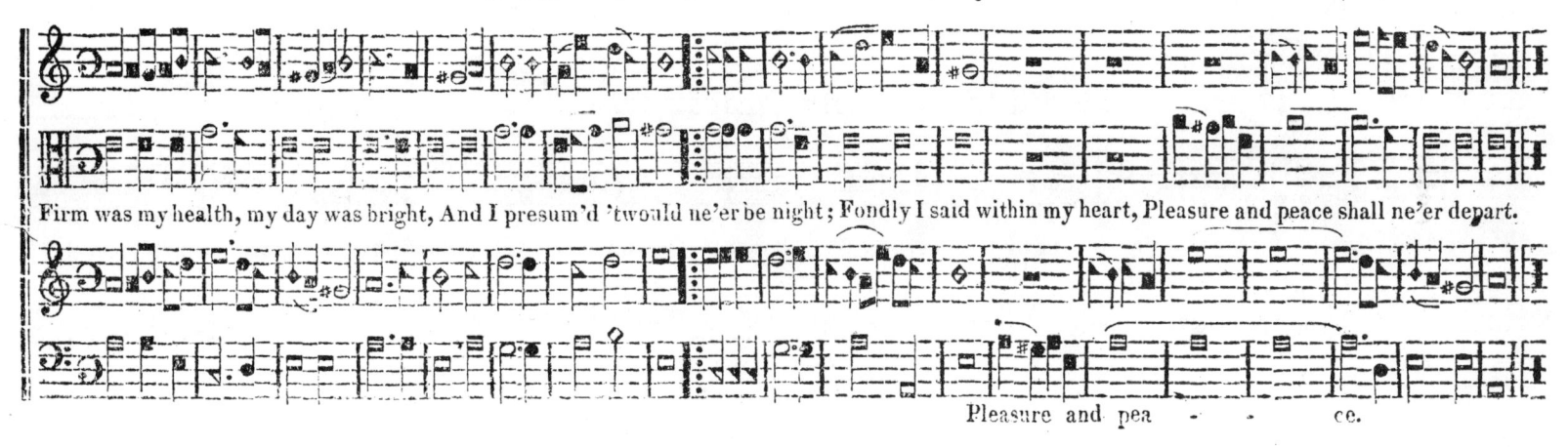

Firm was my health, my day was bright, And I presum'd 'twould ne'er be night; Fondly I said within my heart, Pleasure and peace shall ne'er depart.

Pleasure and pea - - ce.

CHRISTIAN SONG. L. M. Major Key on D.

Mine eyes are now closing to rest, My body must soon be remov'd, And mould'ring, lie buried in dust, No more to be envy'd or lov'd. No more, &c.

Ah! what is this drawing my breath, And stealing my senses away? Oh! tell me, Oh! tell me, my soul, is it death, Releasing me kindly from clay.

Oh! tell me,

Christian Song, continued.

Now, mounting, my soul shall descry, the regions of pleasure and love, My spirit triumphant shall fly, And dwell with my Saviour above.

LIBERTY.   C. M.   Major Key on F.

No more beneath th' oppressive hand Of tyrany we mourn; Behold, the smiling happy land, That freedom calls her own, Behold &c. Behold, That freedom calls her own.

Behold

JUDGMENT ANTHEM. Minor Key on E.

Judgment Anthem, continued.

ro - ll. der cloud,

roll. Hear the sound of Christ victorious, Lo he breaks thro' yon-

Is that he who dy'd on Calv'ry, That was pierced with the

midst ten thousand, :‖: :‖: :‖: saints and angels, see the cru - ci - fi - ed shine.

Judgment Anthem, continued.

spear, Tell us seraphs, you that wonder'd, See he rises thro' the air, Hail him; Oh, Oh

Hail him, Oh, yes 'tis Jesus; Hallelujah, hallelujah, hallelujah,

yes tis Jesus, Oh,

O come quickly, O come quickly, O come quickly, Oh, come quickly, Hallelujah, come, Lord come.

O come quickly, Oh

Judgment Anthem, continued. 63

Happy, happy mourners, happy mourners, happy mourners, Lo, in clouds he comes he comes. Now determin'd ev'ry evil to destroy.

View him smiling,

All ye nations now shall sing him, Songs of everlasting joy ; Now redemption long expected, See the solemn pomp appear : All his people once rejected

Judgment Anthem, continued.

now shall meet him in the air; Hallelujah, hallelujah welcome, welcome, bleeding lamb Now his merit by the harpers, Thro' the eternal deep resound,

Now resplendant shine his nail prints, Ev'ry eye shall see the wound.   They who pierc'd him shall at his appearance wail.

Judgment Anthem, continued.

Ev'ry island, sea & mountain, Heav'n & earth shall flee away; All who hate him must, ashamed, Hear the trump proclaim the day, Come to judgment,

come to judgment, come to judgment, Stand before the Son of man. Hark, hark, the archangel swe - - lls the solemn summons loud.

Judgment Anthem, Continued.

Tears the strong pillars of the vault of heav'n, Breaks up old marble the repose of princes; See the graves open & the bones arising, Flames all around them.
Hark the shrill outcries of the guilty wretches, Lively bright horror and amazing anguish Stare thro' their eyelids, While the living worm Lies gnawing within them.

See the judge's hand arising, Fill'd with vengeance on his foes;

Down to hell there's no redemption, Ev'ry Christless soul must go, Down to hell, depart, depart, depart, ye cursed into ever-

Judgment Anthem, continued.

Hear the Savior's words of mercy, Come you ransom'd sinners home; Swift and joyful in your journey, To the palace of your God.

lasting flames.

See the souls that earth des-
Joy celestial hymns harmo-

pised, in celestial glories move: Hallelujah big with wonder, Praising Christ's eternal love: Hallelujah, hallelujah echo thro the realms of light.
nious in soft symphony resound, Angels, seraphs, harps and trumpets Swell the sweet angelic sound; Hail Almighty :||: Great eternal Lord, Amen.

CASTLE STREET. L. M. Major Key on G.

Sweet is the work my God my King, To praise thy name give thanks & sing; To show thy love by morning light, And talk of all thy truth at night.

Continued.

And talk of all. &c.

WARREN. S. M. Major Key on A.

Let all our tongues be one, to praise our God on high; Who from his bosom sent his Son To fetch us strangers nigh.

CONTENT. S. M. Minor Key on A.

Since God is all my trust, A refuge always nigh. Why should I like a tim'rous bird, Why, &c. Why, &c. To distant mountains fly.

Continued.

To distant, &c.

WALSAL. C. M. Minor Key on A.

Alas! and did my Sav'.r bleed? And did my Sov'reign die? Would he devote that sacred head, For such a a wretch as I?

HUNDRED & FORTY-EIGHTH. L. M. Major Key on G.

Loud hallelujahs to the Lord, From distant worlds where creatures dwell; Let heav'n begin the solemn word, And sound it dreadful down to hell. Let heav'n, &c.

The Lord how absolute he reigns, Let ev'ry angel bend the knee;

Hundred and Forty-Eighth, continued.

71

world, O

Sing of his love in heav'nly strains, And speak how fierce his terrors be. High on a throne his glories dwell, An awful throne of shining bliss; Fly thro the

Continued

sun, & tell, how dark thy beams compar'd to his.

LANDAFF. S. M. Minor Key on A.

Slow.

Let sinners take their course, And choose the road to death, But in the worship of my God,

I'll spend my daily breath.

THANKSGIVING ANTHEM. Major Key on C.

O be joyful in the Lord, all ye la - - - nds, Serve the Lord with gladness, Serve, &c.

O be joyful in the Lord, O be joyful in the Lord, O be joyful in the Lord, all ye lands,

Serve the Lord with gladness, And come before his presence, And come, &c. with a song. Be ye sure that the Lord he is God. Be ye sure &c.

Thanksgiving Anthem, continued.

We are his people, we &c.   and the sheep of his pasture.   We   and the

It is he that has made us, and not we ourselves.   We are his people, and the sheep of his pasture, We are his people, We are &c.

We are his people and the sheep of his pasture.

DUET—Counter and Bass.   Very slow.

O   go   your   way   in - to   his   gates, with thanksgiving, with thanksgiving, and   in - to his   courts   with praise. Be thankful   unto   him,   be   thankful   un - to   him, And   speak,   speak good   of his name.

Thanksgiving Anthem, Continued.

For the lord is gracious, for the Lord is gracious, And his mercy is everlasting, and his mercy is everlasting, everlasting, and his mercy is

everlasting, everlasting, and his mercy is everlasting, everlasting, And his truth endureth from generation to generation.

Thanksgiving Anthem, continued.

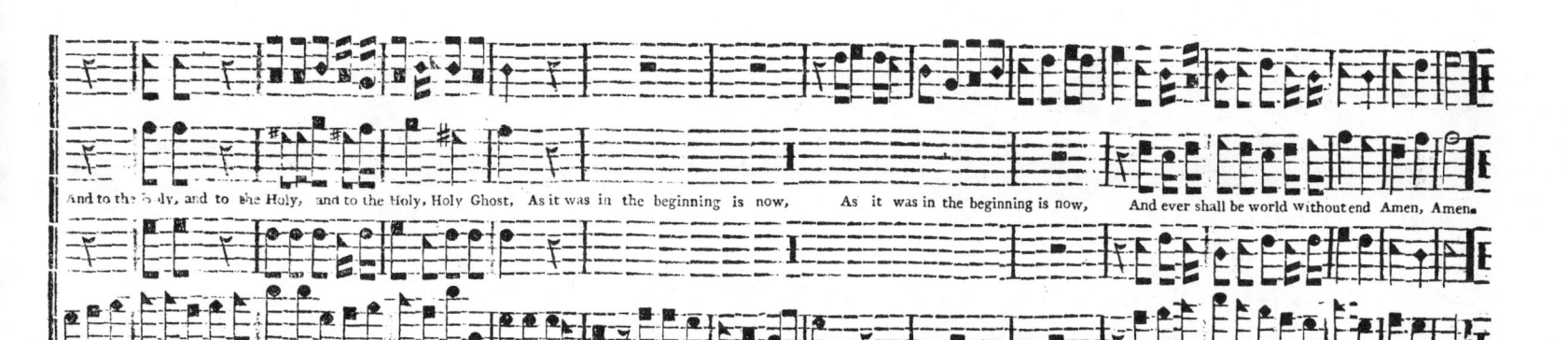

Distinctly and moderate.   *Lively.*

And his truth endureth from generation to generation.   Glory be to the Father, & to the Son, & to the Holy Ghost, Glory be to the Father & to the Son,

And to the Holy, and to the Holy, and to the Holy, Holy Ghost, As it was in the beginning is now,   As it was in the beginning is now,   And ever shall be world without end Amen, Amen.

INTERROGATION S. M. Minor Key on E.

Shall we go on to sin, Because thy grace abounds, Because thy grace abounds, Or crucify the Lord again, And open all his wounds? Or crucify &c.

Continued.

And open all his wounds.

SOLITUDE. C. M. Minor Key on A.

Come lead me to some lonely shade. Where turtles moan their loves; Tall shadows were for lovers made, And grief becomes the groves.

BOSTON. C. M. Major Key on F. 77

My trust is in my heav'nly friend, My hope in thee, my God; Rise, and my helpless life defend, Rise &c.

Rise, and my helpless life defend, From those that seek my blood Rise, and my helpless life defend, From those that seek my blood

Rise, and my helpless life defend, From those that seek my blood, From those that seek my blood. Rise &c.

Continued

From those that seek my blood.

From those

NEWMARK. C. M. Major Key on G.

Come, holy Spirit, heav'nly Dove, With all thy quick'ning pow'rs Kindle a flame of sacred love, In these cold hearts of ours.

SOUNDING JOY. C. M. Major Key on D.

Joy to the earth the Savior reigns; Let men their songs employ; While Repeat &c.

While &c.

While fields & floods, rocks, hills and plains, repeat the sounding j - - - oy,

Continued.

Repeat

DEPENDENCE. S. M. Minor Key on A.

But I with all my care, Will lean upon the Lord;

I'll cast my burdens on his arm, And rest upon his word. And rest &c.

REDEEMING GRACE. 9 & 8. Major Key on G.

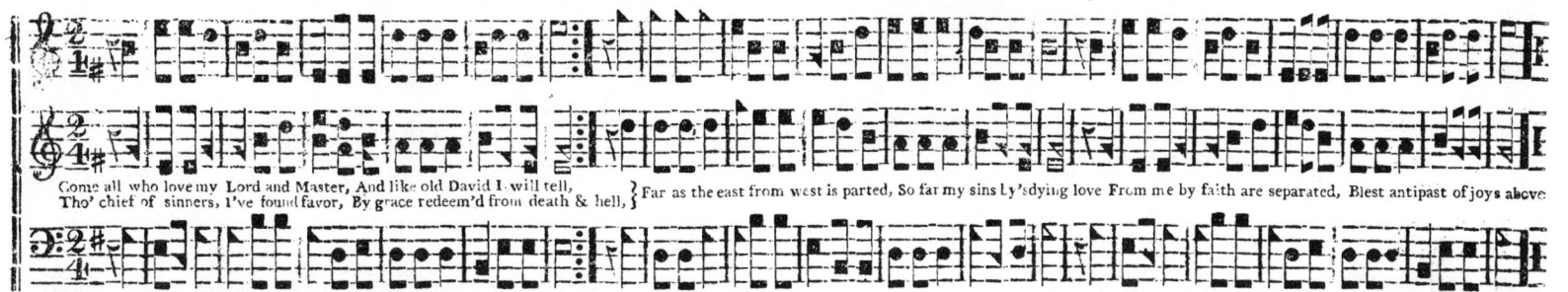

Come all who love my Lord and Master, And like old David I will tell,
Tho' chief of sinners, I've found favor, By grace redeem'd from death & hell,
Far as the east from west is parted, So far my sins Ly'sdying love From me by faith are separated, Blest antipast of joys above

I late estrang'd—from Jesus wand'red,
And thought each dang'rous poison good;
But he in mercy long pursu'd me,
With cries of his redeeming blood.
Though like Bartim'ous I was blinded
In nature's darkest light concealed,
But Jesus' love remov'd my blindness,
And he his pard'ning grace reveal'd.

Now I will serve him while he spares me,
And with his people sing aloud;
Though hell oppose and sinners mock me,
In rapt'rous songs I'll praise my God.
By faith I view the heav'nly concert
They sing high strains of Jesus' love
Oh! with desire my soul is longing
And fain would be with Christ above.

That blessed day is fast approaching,
When Christ in glorious clouds will come,
With sounding trumps & shouts of angels
To call each faithful spirit home
There's Ab'ram, Isaac, holy prophets,
And all the saints at God's right hand
There hosts of angels join in concert
Shout as they reach the promis'd land.

CHRISTMAS HYMN. 11's. Major Key on G.

A virgin unspotted the prophets foretold,
Should bring forth a Savior which now we behold;
To be our Redeemer from Death, hell & sin, Which Adam's transgression involved us in.
Then let us be merry, cast sorrows away Our Savior Christ Jesus was born on this day.

TRIUMPH. 11's. Major Key on C

Tis done! lo they come, bright celestials descend, Saints, angels, and seraphs, their symphonies lend; } Cease! cease, then fond nature, oh! cease
The spheres are all vocal, the raptures draw near, Impartial vibrations resound in my ear. then thy strife,

And let me now languish and die into life. Blest powers receive me, I mount on your wing, O grave where's thy vict'ry, O death where's thy sting.

DAVIS. 11 & 8. Major Key on G.

O thou in whose presence my soul takes delight, On whom in afflictions I call, My comfort by day and my song in the night, My hope my salvation, my all.

2. Where dost thou at noontide resort with thy sheep, To feed on the pastures of love, For why in the valley of death should I weep, Alone in the wilderness rove.
3. O why should I wander an alien from thee, Or cry in the desert for bread, My foes would rejoice when my sorrows they see, And smile at the tears I have shed.
4. Ye daughters of Zion declare, have you seen The star that on Israel shone, Say if in your tents my beloved hath been, And where with his flocks he has gone.
5. This is my beloved, his form is divine, His vestments shed odours around, The locks on his head are as grapes on the vine When autumn with plenty is crown'd
6. The roses of Sharon, the lilies that grow, In vales, on the banks of the streams, His cheeks in the beauty of excellence blow, His eyes all invitingly beams.
7. His voice as the sound of a dulcimer sweet, Is heard thro' the shadows of death, The cedars of Lebanon bow at his feet, The air is perfum'd with his breath.
8. His lips as a fountain of righteousness flow, That waters the garden of grace, From which their salvation the Gentiles shall know, And bask in the smiles of his face.
9. Love sits in his eyelids and scatters delight Thro all the bright mansions on high, Their faces the cherubims veil in his sight. And tremble with fullness of joy.
10. He looks, and ten thousand of angels rejoice, And myriads wait for his word, He speaks, and eternity fill'd with his voice, Re-echoes the praise of her Lord.

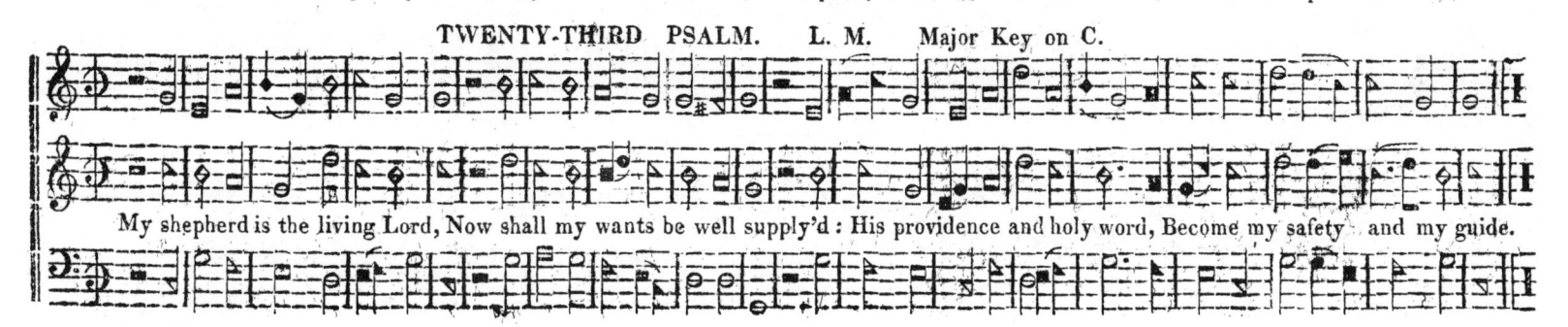

TWENTY-THIRD PSALM. L. M. Major Key on C.

My shepherd is the living Lord, Now shall my wants be well supply'd: His providence and holy word, Become my safety and my guide.

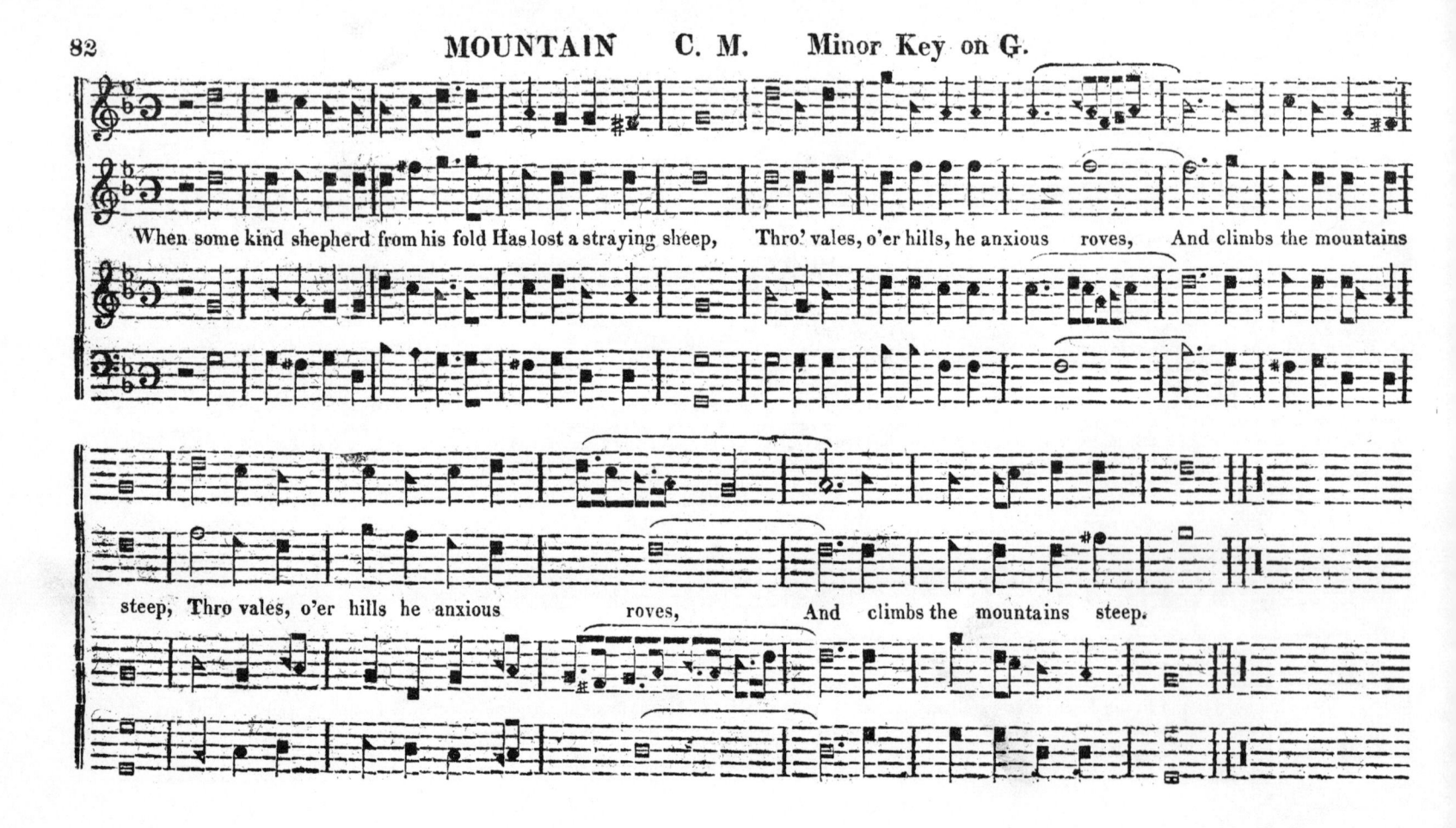

MOUNTAIN C. M. Minor Key on G.

When some kind shepherd from his fold Has lost a straying sheep, Thro' vales, o'er hills, he anxious roves, And climbs the mountains steep, Thro vales, o'er hills he anxious roves, And climbs the mountains steep.

LAMENTATION. L. M. Minor Key on E.

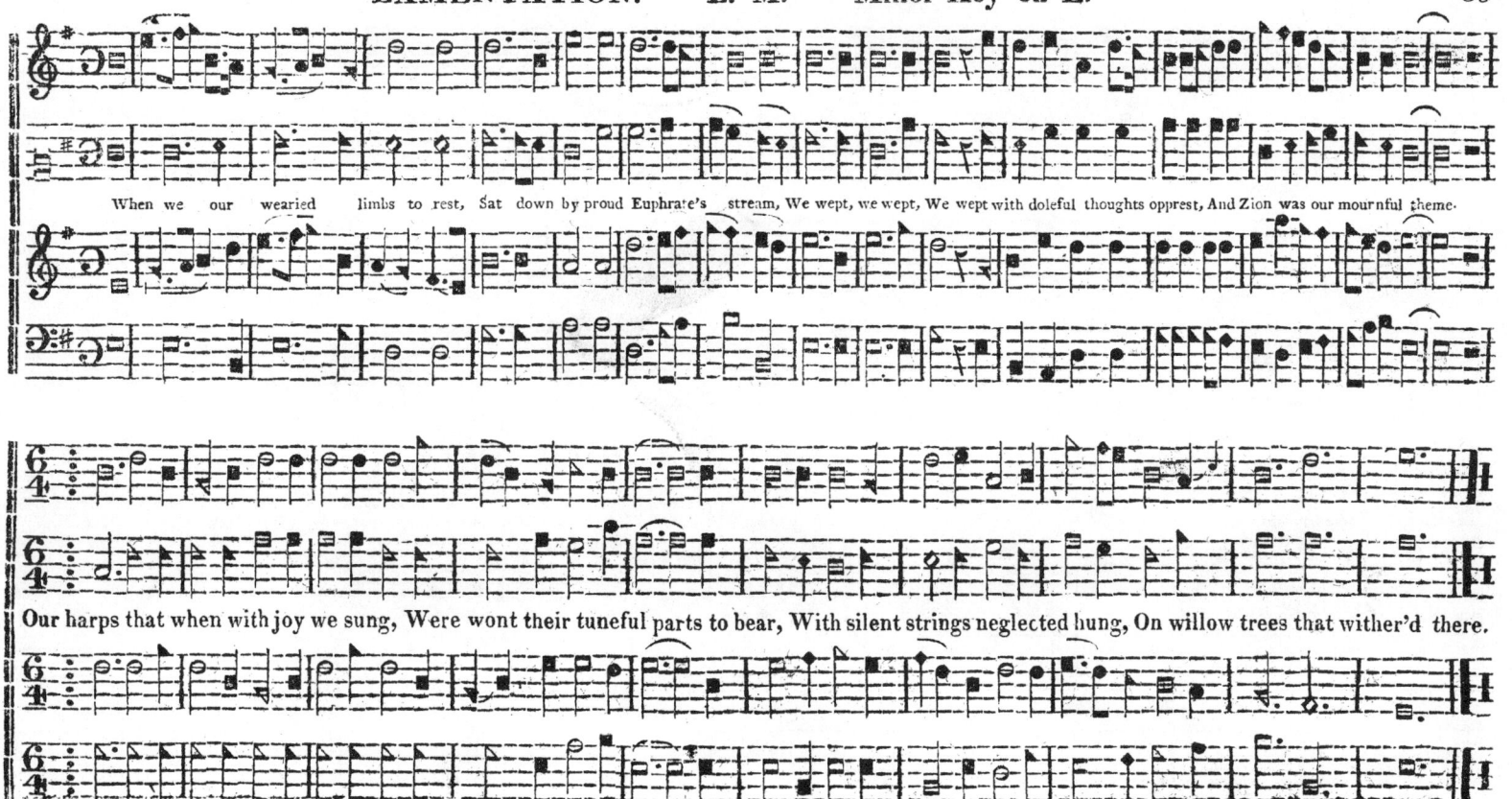

When we our wearied limbs to rest, Sat down by proud Euphrate's stream, We wept, we wept, We wept with doleful thoughts opprest, And Zion was our mournful theme.

Our harps that when with joy we sung, Were wont their tuneful parts to bear, With silent strings neglected hung, On willow trees that wither'd there.

FAREWELL ANTHEM. Minor Key on A.

84

Farewell Anthem Continued.

85

Ne-ver to re-turn. I am go-ing a long journey, never to return. Fare you well, my friends, fare you well, my friends. Fare you well.

to re-turn, never, never, ne-ver, never, never to re-turn, Fare you well, fare you well, my friends. Fare you well, my friends.

turn, never, never, never, never to re-turn. Fare you well, my friends.

never to re-turn, vever, never to re-turn. Fare you you well.

Fare you well my friends, And God grant we may meet together in that world above, Where trouble shall cease, and harmony shall abound.

Farewell Anthem, continued.

hark! hark, my dear friends, for death hath called me, And I must go & lie down in the cold & silent grave, Where the mourners cease from mourning,

and the pris'ner is set free, Where the rich and the poor are both alike. Fare you well! fare you well! fare you well! fare you well! fare you well, my friends.

VERGENNES. C. M. Minor Key on G.

My heart & flesh cry out for thee, While far from thine abode; When shall I tread thy courts & see, My Savior and my God? The sparrow builds her-

self a nest, And suffers no remove, O make me like the sparrow blest, To dwell but where I love. O make &c.

ALL SAINTS NEW. L. M. Minor Key on D.

Oh! if my Lord would come & meet, My soul should stretch her wings in haste, Fly fearless thro' death's iron gate, Nor feel the terrors as she pass'd

Jesus can make a dying bed Feel soft, as downy pillows are, While on his breast I lean While on his breast I lean.

Jesus can &c. While

Jesus can make a dying &c. While And breathe

Jesus can make a dying bed, Feel soft as downy pillows are, While on his breast I lean my head, And breathe my life out sweetly there.

All Saints New, Continued.

89

I lean my head, And breathe, And breathe, And breathe, And breathe my

I lean my head, And breathe, And breathe, And breathe, And breathe my life; And breathe my life out sweetly there.

While on his breast I lean, I lean my head, And breathe my life out sweetly there And breathe

And breathe, And breathe, And

H 2

MARCUS HOOK. C. M. Major Key on C.

Let age to age, &c.

Sweet is the mem'ry of thy grace, My God, my heav'nly King; Let age to age thy righteousness, thy righteousness, In sounds of glory sing. In &c.

Let age Let age In sounds In

EXHORTATION. C. M. Major Key on F.

Lord, in the morning thou shalt hear, My voice ascending high; To thee will I direct my prayer, To the lift up mine eye. To thee &c.

HINSDALE. C. M. Major Key on G.

Thou wilt reveal the paths of life, And raise me to thy throne, Thy courts immortal pleasures give, Thy presence joys unknown.

Thy courts immortal pleasure, pleasure give, Thy

Thy courts immortal pleasure give, Thy courts Thy

WORCESTER. S. M. Major Key on F.

NORTHFIELD. C. M. Major Key on C.

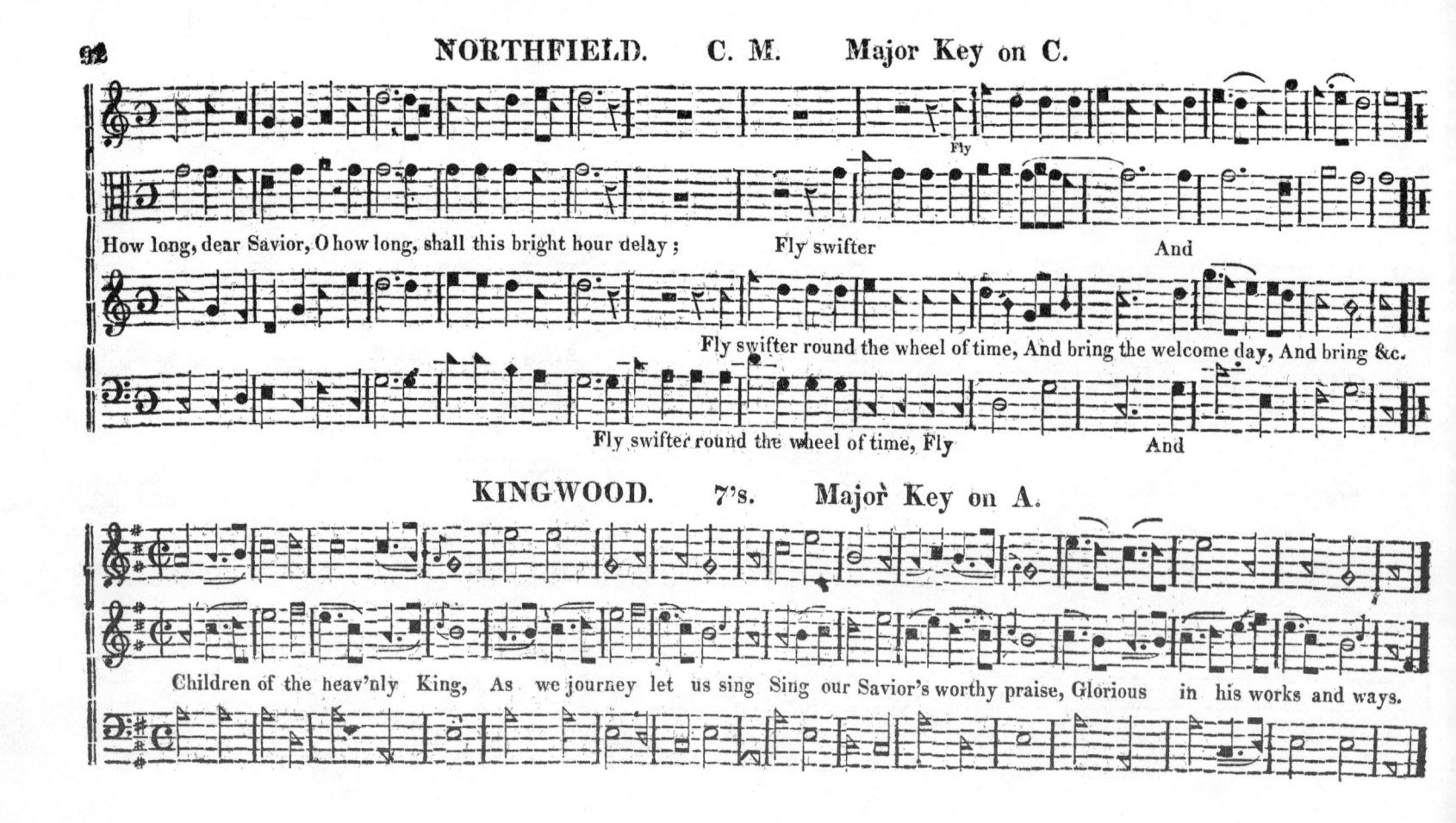

How long, dear Savior, O how long, shall this bright hour delay; Fly swifter And

Fly swifter round the wheel of time, And bring the welcome day, And bring &c.

Fly swifter round the wheel of time, Fly And

KINGWOOD. 7's. Major Key on A.

Children of the heav'nly King, As we journey let us sing Sing our Savior's worthy praise, Glorious in his works and ways.

PARDONING GRACE. L. M. Minor Key on C.

From deep distress & troubled thoughts, To thee, my God, I rais'd my cries: If thou severely mark our faults, No flesh can stand before thine eyes.

Continued.

MILES's LANE. C. M. Major Key on C.

All hail the pow'r of Jesus' name, Let saints and angels fall; Bring forth the royal diadem, And crown him, :||: :||: :||: Lord of all.

2. Crown him, ye martyrs of our God, Who from his altar call; Extol the stem of Jesse's rod, And crown him Lord of all.
3. Ye Gentile sinners, ne'er forget, The wormwood and the gall; Go spread your trophies at his feet, And crown him Lord of all.
4. Let ev'ry kindred, ev'ry tribe On this terrestrial ball, To him all majesty ascribe, And crown him Lord of all.
5 O that, with yonder sacred throng, We at his feet may fall, To join in everlasting song, And crown him Lord of all.

SPRINGHILL. P. M. Major Key on G.

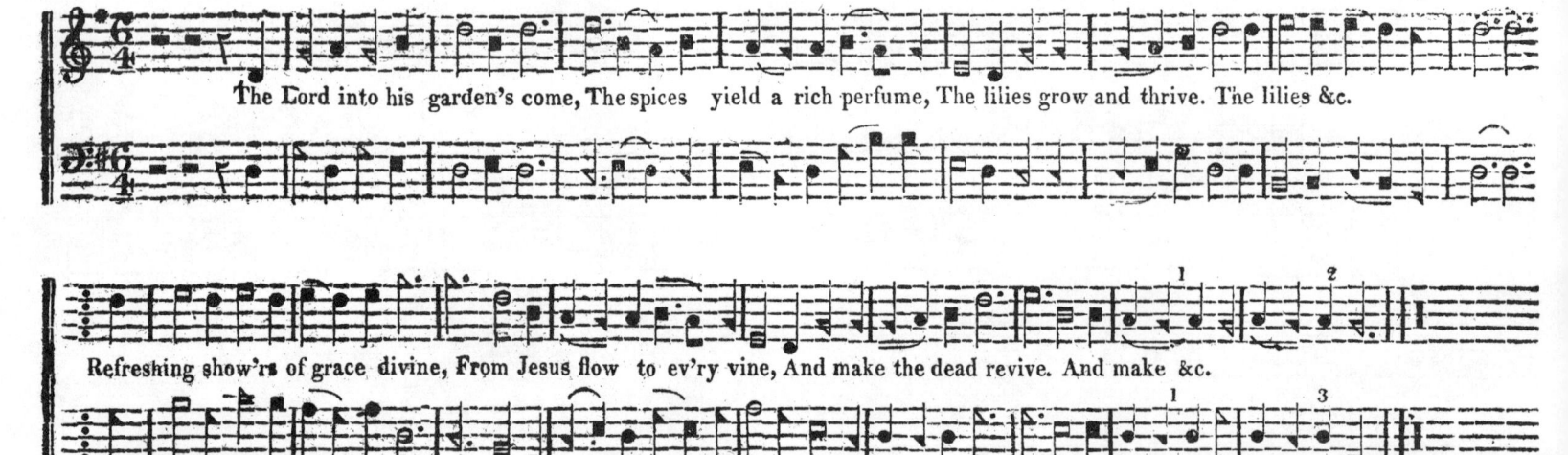

The Lord into his garden's come, The spices yield a rich perfume, The lilies grow and thrive. The lilies &c.

Refreshing show'rs of grace divine, From Jesus flow to ev'ry vine, And make the dead revive. And make &c.

2 O that this dry and barren ground,
In springs of water may abound;
  A fruitful soil become:
The desert blooming as the rose,
When Jesus conquers all his foes,
  And makes his people one.
3 The glorious time is coming on,
The gracious work is now begun,
  My soul a witness is;
I taste and see the pardon free,
For all mankind as well as me;
  Who come to Christ may live.

4 The worst of sinners here may find
A Savior merciful and kind,
  Who will them all receive;
None are too vile who will repent,
Out of one sinner legions went,
  The Lord did him relieve. [Lord,
5 Come, brethren dear, who know the
And taste the sweetness of his word,
  In Jesus's ways go on;
Our troubles and our trials here.
Will only make us richer there,
  When we arrive at home.

6 We feel that heav'n is now begun,
It issues from the sparkling throne,
  From Jesus throne on high;
It comes in floods we can't contain,
We drink, and drink, and drink again,
  And yet we still are dry.
7 But when we come to dwell above,
And all surround the throne of love,
  We'll drink a full supply;
Jesus will lead his armies through,
To living fountains were they flow,
  That never will run dry.

8 Tis' there we'll reign, & shout & sing,
And make the upper regions ring
  When all the saints get home;
Come on, come on, my brethren dear,
Soon we shall meet together there,
  For Jesus bids us come.
9 Amen, Amen, my soul replies,
I'm bound to meet him in the skies,
  And claim my mansion there:
Now here's my heart, & here's my hand,
To meet you in that heav'nly land,
  Where we shall part no more.

ROCKBRIDGE L. M. Major Key on C.

Far from my thoughts vain world be gone, Let my relig'ous hours alone; Fain would my eyes my Savior see, I wait a visit Lord from thee

SAINT MICHAEL's. P. M. Major Key C.

O praise ye the Lord, Prepare your glad voice, His praise in the great assembly to sing; In their great Creator Let all men rejoice, And heirs of salvation Be glad in their King.

INVITATION. L. M. Major Key of D.

Come my beloved haste away, Cut short the hours of thy delay, Fly like a youthful hart or roe, Over the hills were spices grow.

Fly like a youthful hart or roe, Over the hills where spices grow Over the hills where spices grow.

Fly like a youthful hart or roe. Over the hills where spices grow, Fly

roe, Over   Fly   Over

ROCKINGHAM. C. M. Major Key on A.

Salvation! O the joyful sound, What pleasure to our ears; A sov'reign balm for ev'ry wound, A cordial for our fears.

UNITIA. 10. 11. 10. 11. Major Key on G.

O tell me no more of this world's vain store, The time for such trifles with me now is o'er. A country I've found, where true joys abound, To dwell I'm determin'd on that happy ground.

GANGES. 8. 8. 6. Major Key on D.

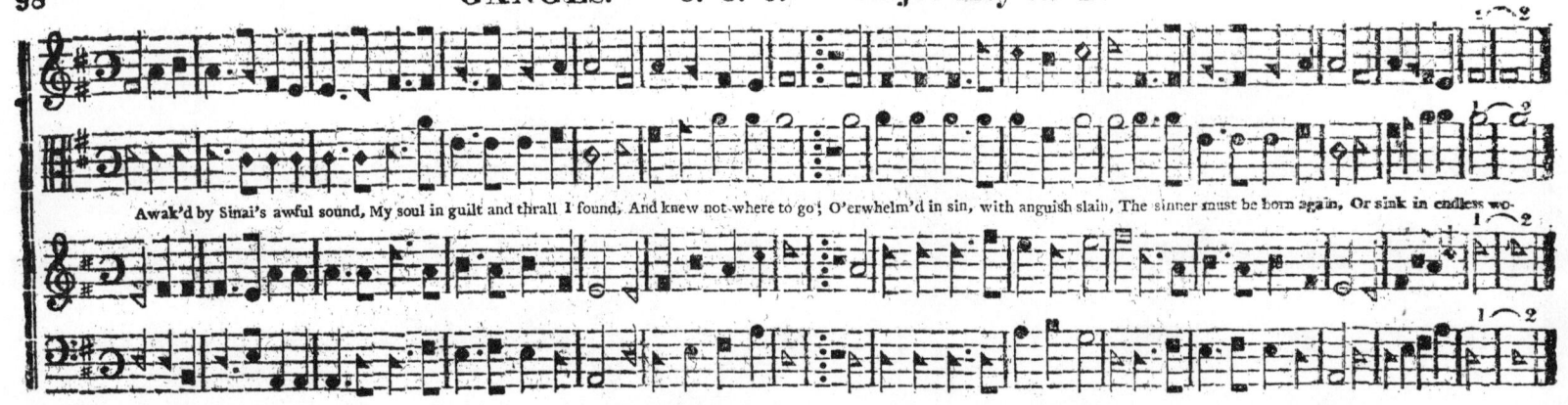

Awak'd by Sinai's awful sound, My soul in guilt and thrall I found, And knew not where to go; O'erwhelm'd in sin, with anguish slain, The sinner must be born again, Or sink in endless wo-

2 Amaz'd I stood but could not tell Which way to shun the way to hell, For death and hell drew near; I strove indeed but strove in vain, The sinner must be born again, Still sounded in my ear.
3 When to the law I trembling fled, It pour'd its curses on my head I no relief could find; This fearful truth increas'd my pain, The sinner must be born again, O'erwhelm'd my tortured mind.
4 Again did Sinai's thunder roll, And guilt lay heavy on my soul, A vast unwieldy load; Alas I read and saw it plain the sinner must be born again, Or drink the wrath of God.
5 The saints I heard with rapture tell, How Jesus conquer'd death and hell, And broke the fowler's snare; Yet when I found this truth remain, The sinner must be born again, I sunk in deep despair.
6 But while I thus in anguish lay, Jesus of Nazareth pass'd that way, And felt his pity move; The sinner by his justice slain, Now by his grace is born again, And sings redeeming love.
7 To heaven the joyful tidings flew, The angels tun'd their harps anew, And lofty notes did raise; All hail the Lamb that once was slain, Unnumber'd millions born again, Still shout thine endless praise.

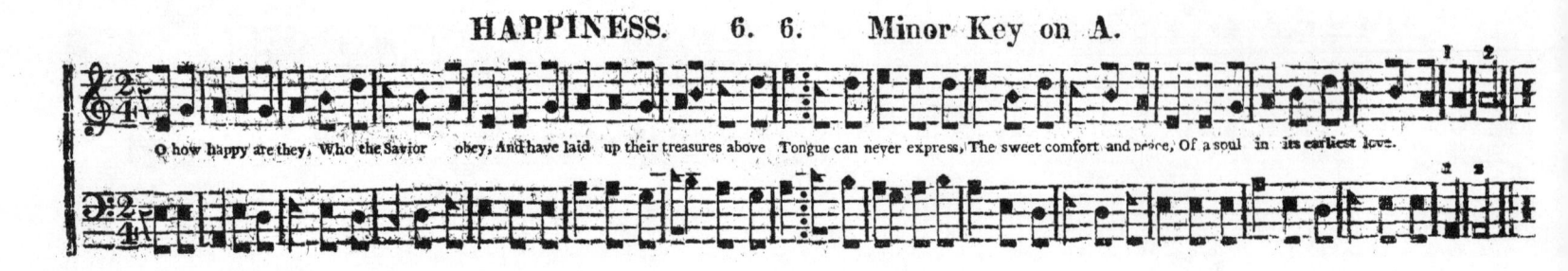

HAPPINESS. 6. 6. Minor Key on A.

O how happy are they, Who the Savior obey, And have laid up their treasures above Tongue can never express, The sweet comfort and peace, Of a soul in its earliest love.

THE BAND OF LOVE. Duetto. Major Key on G.

Our souls by love to-gether knit, Cemented mix'd in one; One hope, one heart, one mind, one voice, 'Tis heav'n on earth begun. Our hearts have burn'd while Jesus spoke. And glow'd with sacred fire. He stop'd, and talk'd, and fed, and bless'd. And fill'd th' enlarg'd desire. A Saviour let creation sing. A Saviour let all heaven ring. He's God with us. We feel him ours. His fulness in our souls he pours. 'Tis almost done, 'Tis almost o'er. We're joining them who are gone before, We soon shall meet to part no more. We soon shall meet to part no more.

2. The little cloud increases still, The heav'ns are big with rain; We haste to catch the teeming show'r, And all its moisture drain.
A rill, a stream, a torrent flows, But pour the mighty flood; O sweep the nations, shake the earth, Till all proclaim the God. A Savior, &c.
3. And when thou maks't thy jewels up, And sets thy starry crown, When all thy sparkling gems shall shine, Proclaim'd by thee thine own.
May we, the little band of love, We sinners sav'd by grace; From glory unto glory chang'd, Behold thee face to face. A Savior, &c.

SAINT JOHNS. L. M. Minor Key on G

Where are the mourners saith the Lord, That wait & tremble at my word, That walk in darkness all the day, Come make my name your trust & stay.

POWER. L. M. Minor Key on D.

Death like an overflowing stream, Sweeps us away; our life's a dream, An empty tale, a morning flow'r, cut down and withered in an hour.

WILLINGTON. L. M. Minor Key on A.

Show pity, Lord, O Lord forgive; Let a repenting rebel live; Are not thy mercies large and free; May not a sinner trust in thee.

ADORATION. C. M. Major Key on C.

Thee we adore, eternal name, and humbly own to thee, How feeble is our mortal frame! What dying worms are we!

NEW CANAAN. C. M. Major Key on G.

On Jordan's stormy banks I stand, and cast a wishful eye To Canaan's fair and happy land, Where my possessions lie. Where &c.

SUBLIMITY. C. M. Major Key on A.

Before Jehovah's awful throne, Ye nations bow with sacred joy, Know that the Lord is God alone, He can create and he destroy. He &c.

FRIENDSHIP. 8. 6. 8. 6. 8. 8. 8. 6. Major Key on G.

Friendship to ev'ry willing mind, Opens a heav'nly treasure, There may the sons of sorrow find, Sources of real pleasure, See what employments men pursue, Then you will own my words are true—Friendship alone presents to view, Sources of real pleasure.

2 Poor are the joys that fools esteem
Fading and transitory.
Mirth is as fleeting as a dream
Or a delusive story.
Luxury leaves a sting behind
Wounding the body & the mind.
Only in friendship can we find
Pleasure and solid glory.

3 Learning that boasting glitt'ring thing
Is but just worth possessing,
Riches forever on the wing
Scarce can be call'd a blessing.
Fame like a shadow flies away
Titles and dignity decay.
Nothing but friendship can display
Joys that are freed from trouble.

4 Beauty with all its gaudy shows
Is but a painted bubble,
Short is the triumph wit bestows
Full of deceit and trouble.
Sensual pleasures swell desire
Just as the fuel feeds the fire
Friendship can real bliss inspire
Bliss that is worth possessing.

5 Happy the man that hath a friend
Formed by the God of nature.
Well may he feel and recommend
Friendship for his Creator.
Then let our hearts in friendship join
To let our social pow'rs combine
Rul'd by a passion most divine
Friendship to our Creator.

SHIELDS. C. M. Minor Key on G.

In-fi-nite grief, amazing wo, Behold my bleeding Lord; Hell and the Jews conspir'd his death, And us'd the Roman sword.

MORALITY. Duetto. Major Key on G. 103

While beauty and youth are in their full prime, And folly and fashion effect our whole time, O let not the phantom our wishes engage, Let us live so in youth that we blush not in age.

2 The vain and the young may attend us awhile, But let not their flat'ry our pudence beguile: Let us covet those charms that shall never decay, Nor listen to all that deceivers can say.
3 I sigh not for beauty, nor languish for wealth, But grant me kind providence virtue and health; Then richer than kings and far happier than they My days shall pass swiftly and sweetly away.
4 For when age steals on me, and youth is no more, And the moralist Time shakes his glass at my door; What pleasure in beauty or wealth can I find, My beauty, my wealth, is a sweet peace of mind.
5 That peace I'll preserve it as pure as 'twas given, Shall last in my bosom an earnest of heaven; For virtue and wisdom can warm the cold scene, And sixty can flourish as gay as sixteen.
6 And when I the burden of life shall have borne, And death with his scithe shall cut the ripe corn. Reascend to my God without murmur or sigh, I'll bless the kind summons and lie down and die.

COMMUNION. C. M. Major Key on E.

The King of heav'n his table spreads, And dainties crown the board; Not Paradise with all its joys, Could such delight afford.

Pardon and peace to dying men, And endless life are giv'n, Thro' the rich blood that Jesus shed, To raise the soul to heav'n.

NEW MONMOUTH, 8. 7. 8. 7. Minor Key on A.

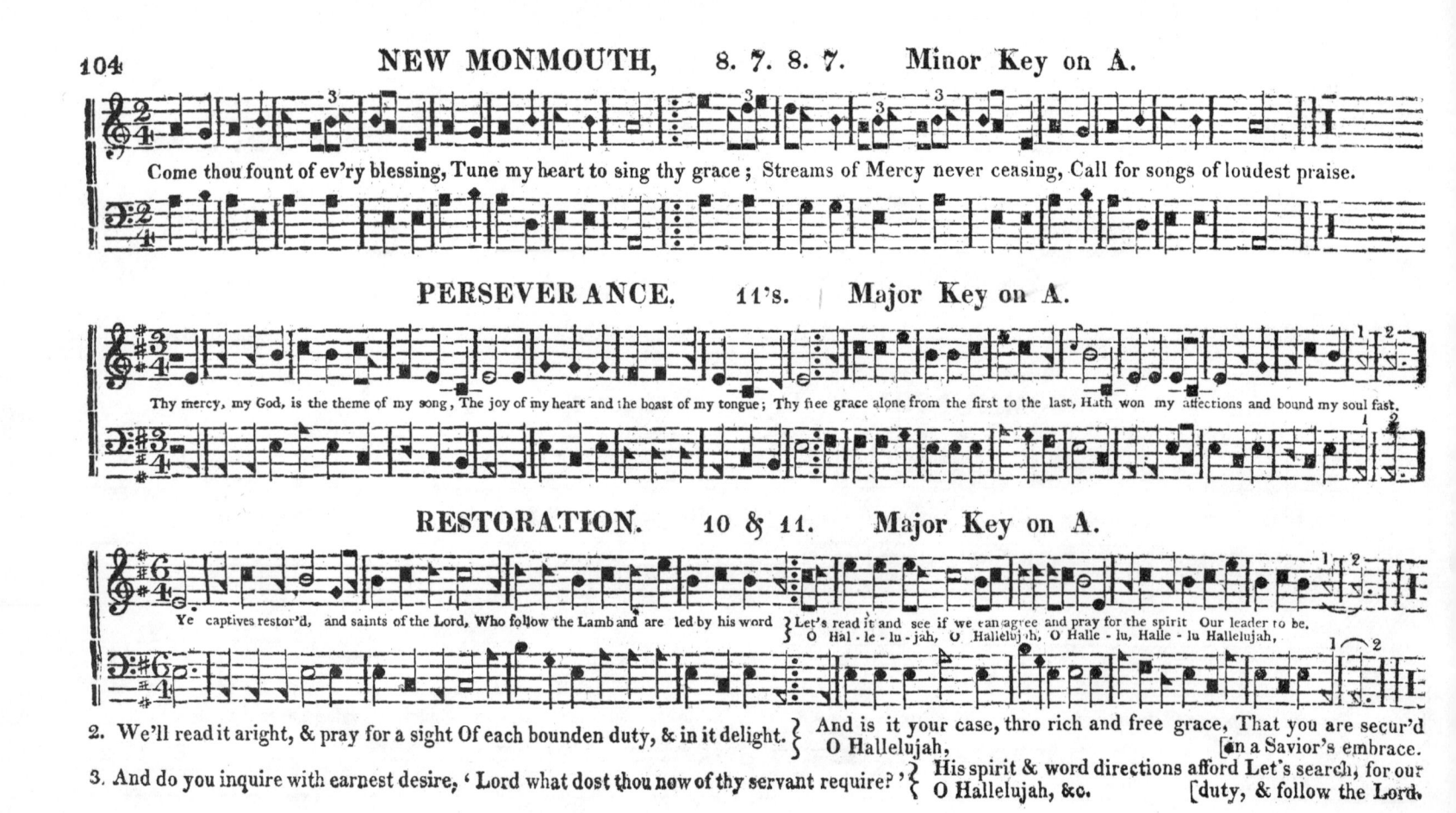

Come thou fount of ev'ry blessing, Tune my heart to sing thy grace; Streams of Mercy never ceasing, Call for songs of loudest praise.

PERSEVERANCE. 11's. Major Key on A.

Thy mercy, my God, is the theme of my song, The joy of my heart and the boast of my tongue; Thy free grace alone from the first to the last, Hath won my affections and bound my soul fast.

RESTORATION. 10 & 11. Major Key on A.

Ye captives restor'd, and saints of the Lord, Who follow the Lamb and are led by his word } Let's read it and see if we can agree and pray for the spirit Our leader to be.
O Hal-le-lu-jah, O Hallelujah, O Halle-lu, Halle-lu Hallelujah,

2. We'll read it aright, & pray for a sight Of each bounden duty, & in it delight. } And is it your case, thro rich and free grace, That you are secur'd
O Hallelujah, [in a Savior's embrace.

3. And do you inquire with earnest desire, 'Lord what dost thou now of thy servant require?' } His spirit & word directions afford Let's search, for our
O Hallelujah, &c. [duty, & follow the Lord.

CONSOLATION. 8's 6 & 8's.   Minor Key on A. 105

Come on my partners in distress, My comrades thro the wilderness, Who still your bodies feel, A while forget your griefs and fears, And look beyond this vale of tears, To that celestial hill. To that celestial hill.

2 Beyond the bounds of time and space Look forward to that heavenly place The saints secure abode. On faith's strong eagles pinions rise And force your passage to the skies And scale the mount of God.
3 Who suffer with our master here We shall before his face appear And by his side sit down. To patient faith the prize is sure And all that to the end endure The cross shall wear the crown.
4 Thrice blessed bliss inspiring hope It lifts the fainting spirits up, It brings to life the dead Our conflicts here shall soon be past, And you and I ascend at last Triumphant with our head.
5 That great mysterious Deity We soon with open face shall see, The beatific sight Shall fill the heavenly courts with praise, And wide diffuse the golden blaze Of everlasting light.
6 The father shining on his throne The glorious coeternal Son The spirit one and seven Conspire in raptures to compleat And lo we fall before his feet And silence heightens heaven.
7 In hopes of that extatic pause Jesus we now sustain the cross And at thy footstool fall Till thou our hidden life reveal Till thou our ravished spirits fill And God is all in all.

VIENNA.   Minor Key on A.

Rise, O Lord our God, Hear our mournful cry; To the world our hearts By our senses chained. If thou dost not change us, All our hopes must die.

Change our stubborn wills Turn us and forgive; Make us hate our sins; Work in us repentance; Show to us the Savior; Say unto us live.

MENDON. Minor Key on A.

My Redeemer, let me be Quite happy at thy feet, Still to know myself and thee, Be this my bitter sweet Look upon my infant state, And with a father's yearnings bless, Don't thy ransom'd child forget, Nor leave him in distress,

THE TRANSPORT. 12. & 11. Major Key on C.

Ye children of Jesus who're bound to the kingdom, Attune all your voices & help me me to sing,
Sweet anthems of praises to my loving Jesus, For he is my prophet, my priest and my king;
When Jesus found me astray I was going.
His love did surround me and sav'd me from ruin He kindly embrac'd me and freely he bless'd me, And taught me aloud his sweet praises to sing.

2 Why should you go mourning from such a physician Who is able and willing your sickness to cure, Come to him believing tho' bad your condition, His father has promised your case to ensure.
My soul he hath heal'd, my heart he rejoices; He brought me to Zion to join the glad voices, I'll serve him, and praise him and always adore him, Till we meet him in heaven where parting is no more.
3 My heart's now in heaven to Jesus ascended, I'm bound to press on to the mark for the prize, And when my temptations and trials are ended, On wings of bright seraphs my soul will arise,
O Christians! I'm happy in this contemplation; My soul it drinks in the sweet streams of salvation, I long to be flying that I may be vieing With the tallest archangel that shouts in the skies.
4 Cheer up, ye dear pilgrims, for Canaan's before you; We'll scale the bright mountains still shouting free grace; On Zions fair borders we'll sing hallelujah, And sit in the smiles of Emanuel's face.
To those who there enter there is no returning, No sorrow nor sighing, no weeping nor mourning, But joyfully feasting and shouting, and singing, All glory to Jesus who bought this free grace.
5 My soul's full of glory, I'll not stay much longer, Bright angels in heaven do v call me away, My spirit in Jesus grows stronger and stronger, My soul now exults to behold the glad day.
O Christians, O Christians, O had you not rather Be now in full glory with your blessed father Where clouds and temptations and pains and vexations Are all lost forever in perfect bright day.
6 This moment the angels are hovering around us, And joining with mortals to praise their sweet king, And, waiting for Jesus to call and to crown us, To make the bright arches of heaven to ring.
There with our dear Savior, we'll meet one another, The wife and the husband, the sister and brother, In the highest measure of lov'es sweetest pleasure, Salvation, thro Jesus, forever we'll sing.

STERLING. S. M. Major Key on E.

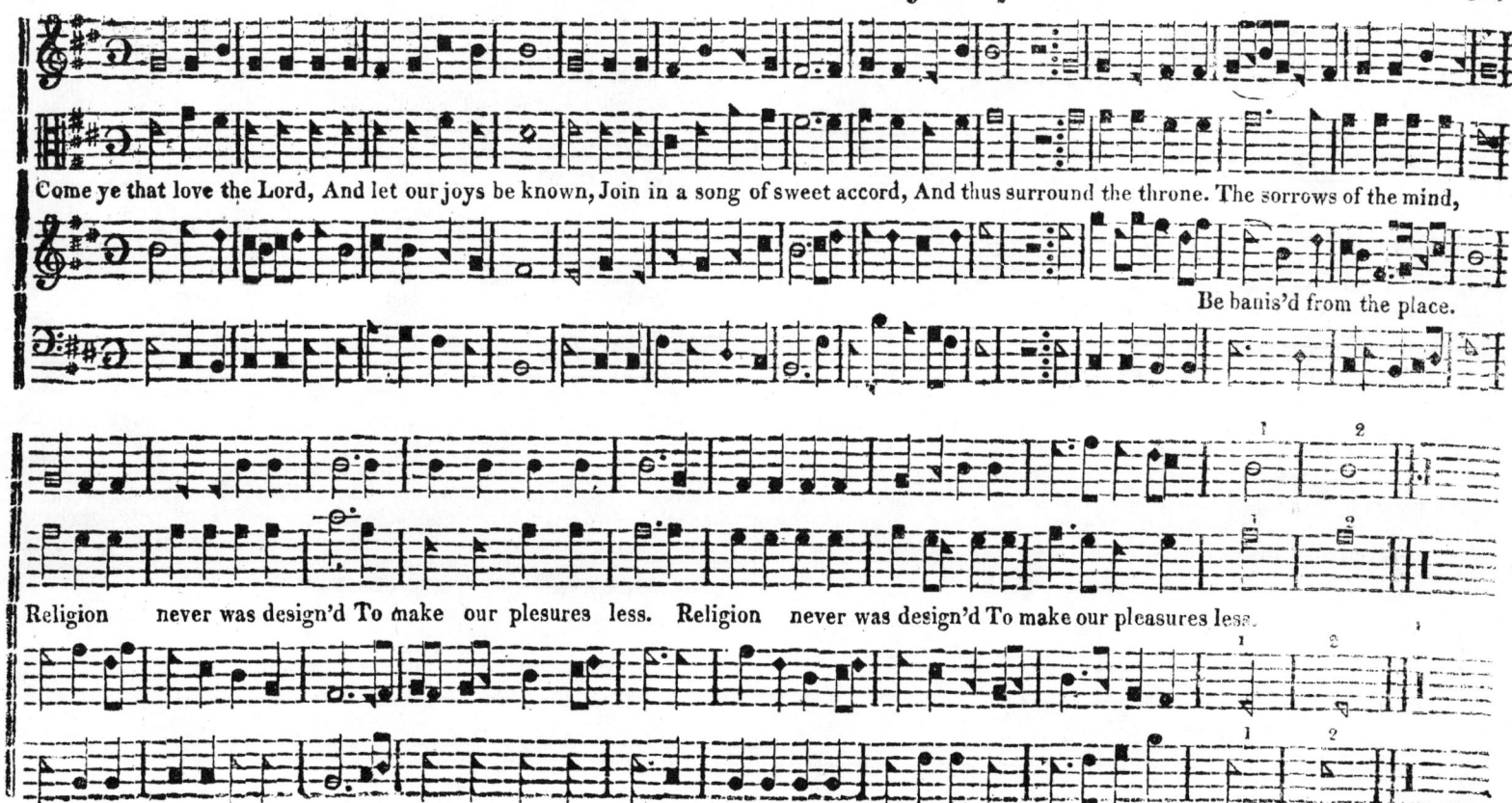

Come ye that love the Lord, And let our joys be known, Join in a song of sweet accord, And thus surround the throne. The sorrows of the mind,

Be banis'd from the place.

Religion never was design'd To make our plesures less. Religion never was design'd To make our pleasures less.

WASHINGTON. L. M. Minor Key on A.

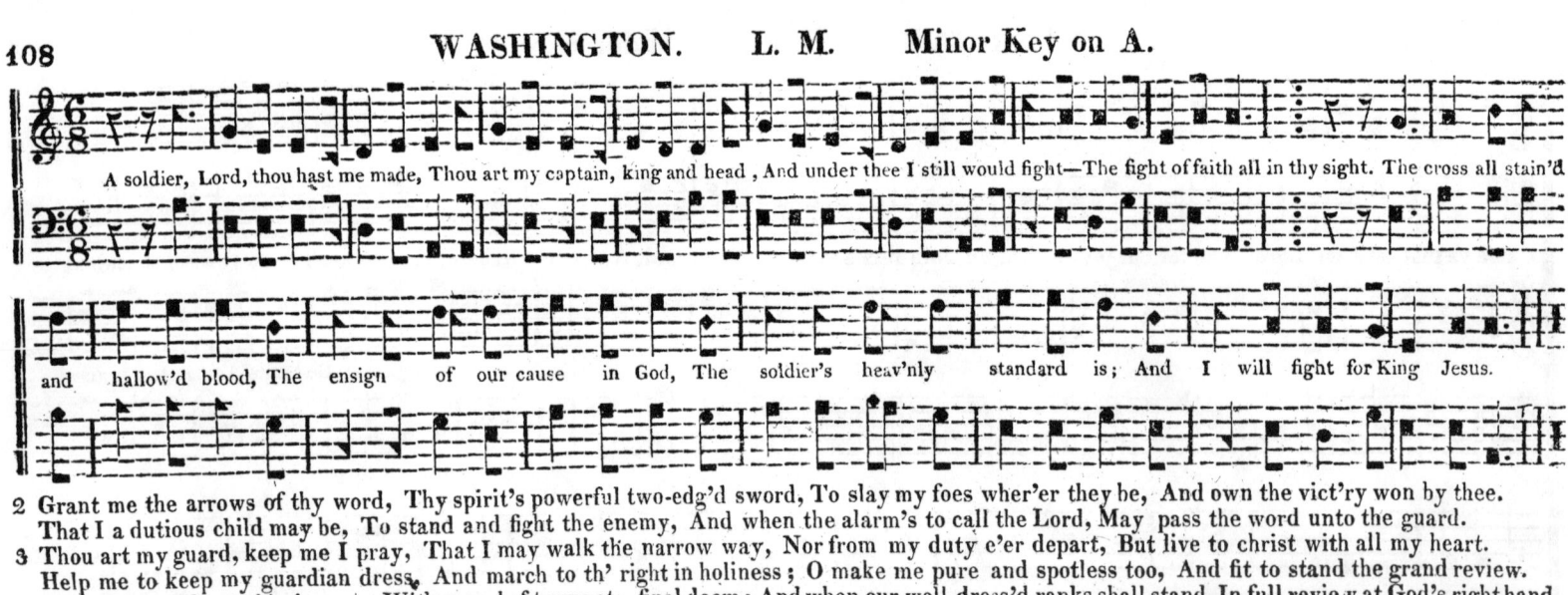

A soldier, Lord, thou hast me made, Thou art my captain, king and head, And under thee I still would fight—The fight of faith all in thy sight. The cross all stain'd and hallow'd blood, The ensign of our cause in God, The soldier's heav'nly standard is; And I will fight for King Jesus.

2 Grant me the arrows of thy word, Thy spirit's powerful two-edg'd sword, To slay my foes wher'er they be, And own the vict'ry won by thee. That I a dutious child may be, To stand and fight the enemy, And when the alarm's to call the Lord, May pass the word unto the guard.

3 Thou art my guard, keep me I pray, That I may walk the narrow way, Nor from my duty e'er depart, But live to christ with all my heart. Help me to keep my guardian dress, And march to th' right in holiness; O make me pure and spotless too, And fit to stand the grand review.

4 And when our Gen'ral he is come, With sound of trumpet—final doom; And when our well-dress'd ranks shall stand, In full review at God's right hand, Its then th' en'my will get the rout, And wheel'd by him to *left about*! Then we'll march up the heavenly street, and ground our arms at JESUS' feet.

ANIMATION. 8 & 7. with Chorus. Major Key on A.

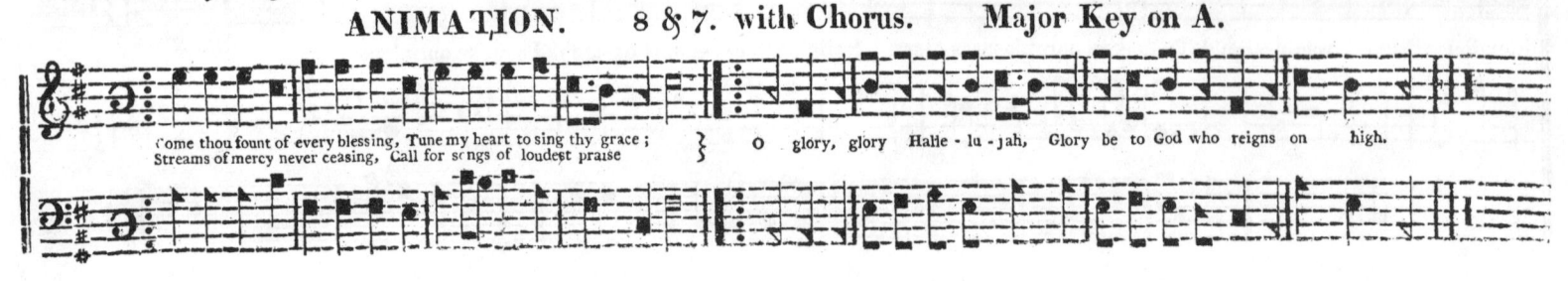

Come thou fount of every blessing, Tune my heart to sing thy grace; Streams of mercy never ceasing, Call for songs of loudest praise O glory, glory Halle-lu-jah, Glory be to God who reigns on high.

MESSIAH. 8 8 8 6 8 8 8 8 6 Minor Key on A. 109

The Son of man they did betray, He was condemn'd and led away; Think, O my soul, that mournful day, Look on Mount Cal-va-ry!

Behold him lamb-like led along, Surrounded by a wicked throng, Accused by each lying tongue, And thus the Lamb of God was hung, Upon the shameful tree.

2 Twas thus the glorious sufferer stood, With hands and feet nail'd to the wood; From ev'ry wound a stream of blood Came trickling down amain;
His bitter groans, all nature struck, And at his voice, the rocks were broke, And sleeping saints their graves forsook. The spiteful Jews had round him mock'd. And laughed at his pain.
3 Thus hung between the earth and skies, Behold him tremble as he dies O sinners! hear his mournful cries; Behold his torturing pain.
The mourning sun withdrew his light, Blush'd and refus'd to own his sight. All azure cloth'd in robes of night, All nature mourn'd and stood affright, When Christ the Lord was slain.
4 Ye men and angels hear the son, He cries for help, but there is none; He treads the wine press all alone, His garments stain'd with blood.
In lamentations hear him cry, Eli lama sabacthany; Tho death may close these languid eyes, He soon will mount the upper skies The conquering son of God
5 Both Jews and Romans in a band, With hearts like steel around him stand. Saying if you're come to save the land, Now try yourself to free-
A soldier pierc'd him when he died, And healing streams came from his side, And thus my Lord was crucify'd, Stern justice now is satisfy'd; Sinners, for you and me.
6 Behold him mount a throne of state, He fills the mediatorial seat, While millions bowing at his feet, In loud hosannas tell;
How he endured exquisite pains, And led the monster death in chains; Ye seraphs raise your highest strains, While music fills bright Salem's plains, He has conquered death and hell.
7 Tis done, the dreadful debt is paid. The great atonement now is made; Sinners on me your guilt was laid For you I spilt my blood;
For you my tender soul did move, For you I left my courts above, That you the length and breadth might prove, The depth and heighth of perfect love, In Christ your smiling God.
8 All Glory be to God on high, who reigns enthron'd above the sky, Who sent his son to bleed and die, Glory to him be given
While heaven above his praise resound, Zion shall sing his grace abound, I hope to sing eternal rounds, In flaming love which knows no bounds When carried up to heav'n.

SOLICITUDE. 11 & 8. Minor Key on G.

O thou in whose presence my soul takes delight, On whom in afflictions I call; My comfort by day and my song in the night, My hope, my salvation, my all.

☞ *For the residue of this hymn, see page 81.*

PASTORAL. L. P. M. Major Key on F.

The Lord my pasture shall prepare, And feed me with a shepherd's care; His presence will my wants supply, And guard me with a watchful eye.

My noon-day walks he will attend, And all my midnight hours defend. And all &c.

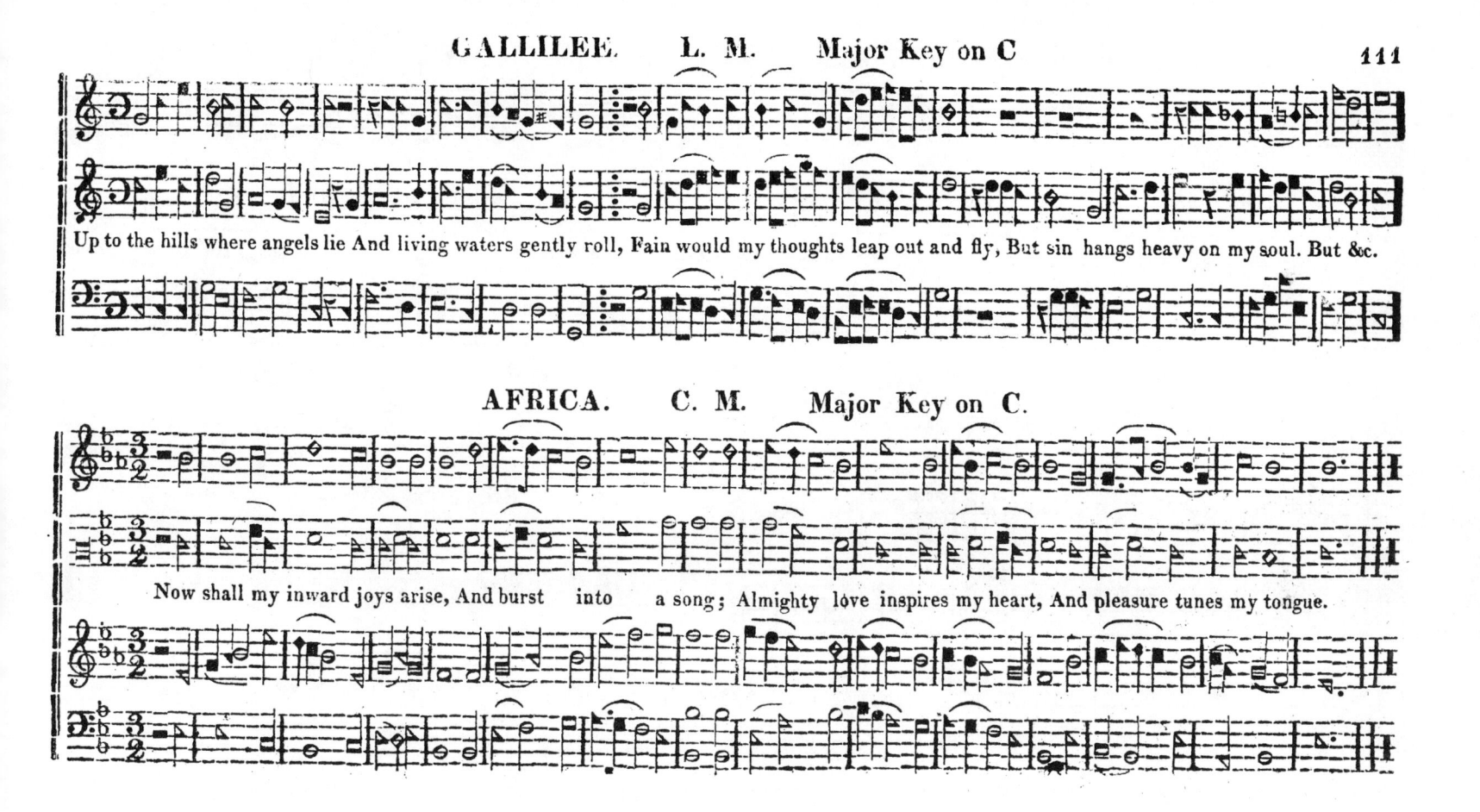

GALLILEE. L. M. Major Key on C

Up to the hills where angels lie And living waters gently roll, Fain would my thoughts leap out and fly, But sin hangs heavy on my soul. But &c.

AFRICA. C. M. Major Key on C

Now shall my inward joys arise, And burst into a song; Almighty love inspires my heart, And pleasure tunes my tongue.

112   PROVIDENCE.   C. M.   Major Key on A.   C. CURTIS.

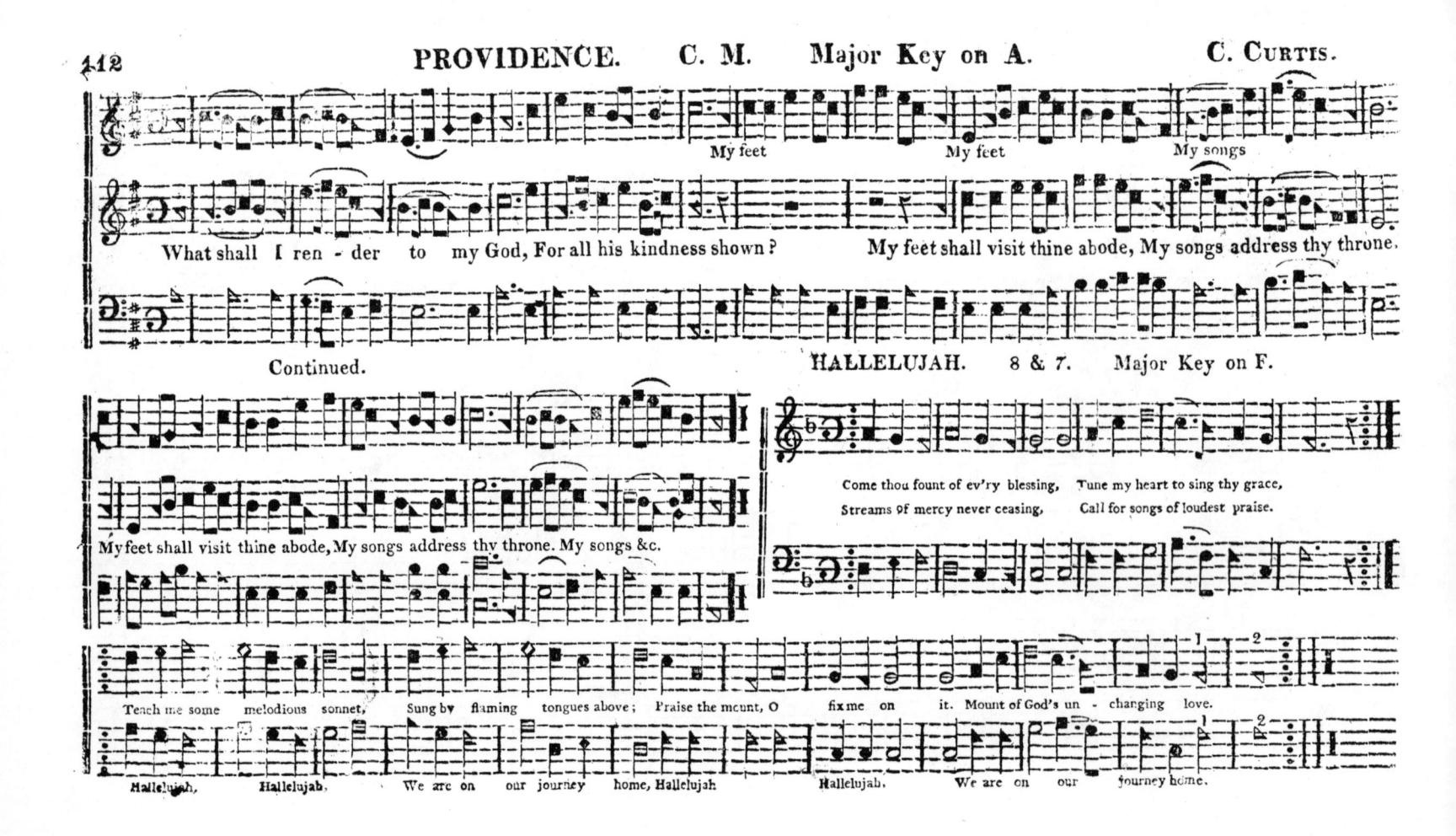

What shall I ren-der to my God, For all his kindness shown? My feet shall visit thine abode, My songs address thy throne.

Continued.

My feet shall visit thine abode, My songs address thy throne. My songs &c.

HALLELUJAH.   8 & 7.   Major Key on F.

Come thou fount of ev'ry blessing, Tune my heart to sing thy grace,
Streams of mercy never ceasing, Call for songs of loudest praise.

Teach me some melodious sonnet, Sung by flaming tongues above; Praise the mount, O fix me on it. Mount of God's un-changing love.

Hallelujah, Hallelujah, We are on our journey home, Hallelujah Hallelujah, We are on our journey home.

CONCERT. 8 & 7. Minor Key on A.

Come thou fount of ev'ry blessing, Tune my heart to sing thy grace, Streams of Mercy ever flowing Call for songs of highest praise.

Teach me some melodious sonnet, Sung by flaming tongues above ; Praise the mount, O fix me on it, Mount of God's unchanging love.

SALFORD. C. M. Minor Key A.

Not from the dust affliction grows, Nor troubles rise, Nor troubles rise by chance ; But we are born But we are born But we are born to cares and woes! A sad inheritance.

114 SEAMAN's SONG. L. M. Major Key on C.

Would you behold the works of God, His wonders in the world abroad, Go with the mariner and trace The unknown regions of the seas. The unknown regions of the seas.

GERMAN HYMN. L. M. Major Key on B.

Very slow.

So fades the lovely blooming flow'r, Frail smiling solace of an hour! So soon our transient comforts fly, And pleasure only blooms to die.

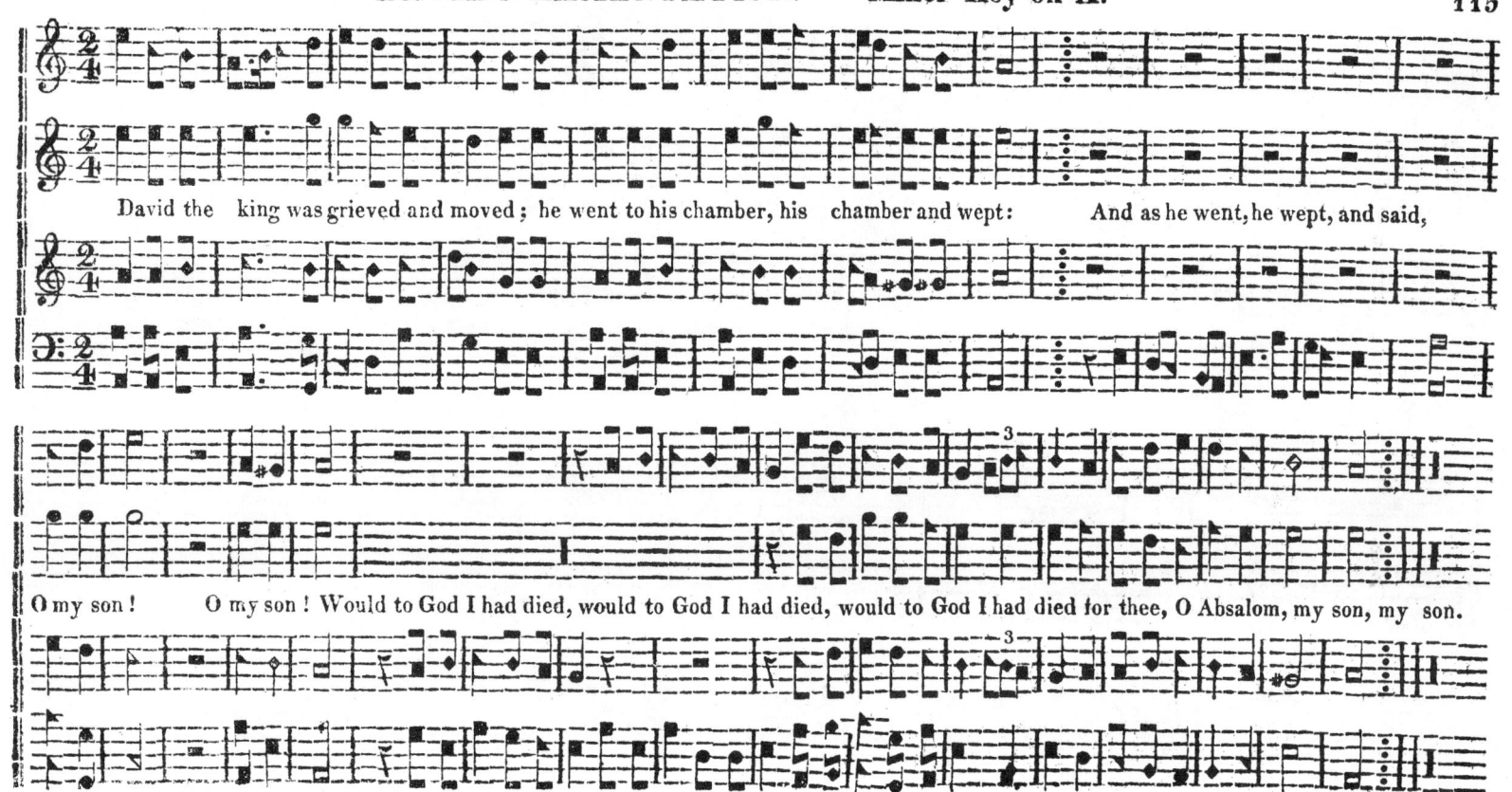

DAVID's LAMENTATION. Minor Key on A.

David the king was grieved and moved; he went to his chamber, his chamber and wept: And as he went, he wept, and said,

O my son! O my son! Would to God I had died, would to God I had died, would to God I had died for thee, O Absalom, my son, my son.

LONSDALE.   S. M.   Major Key on C.

The hill of Zion yields, A thousand sacred sweets, Before we reach the heav'nly fields Or walk the golden streets. Then let our songs abound, And ev'ry tear be dry. We're marching to Immanuel's ground To fairer worlds on high.

SPALDWIC   S. M.   Minor Key on A.

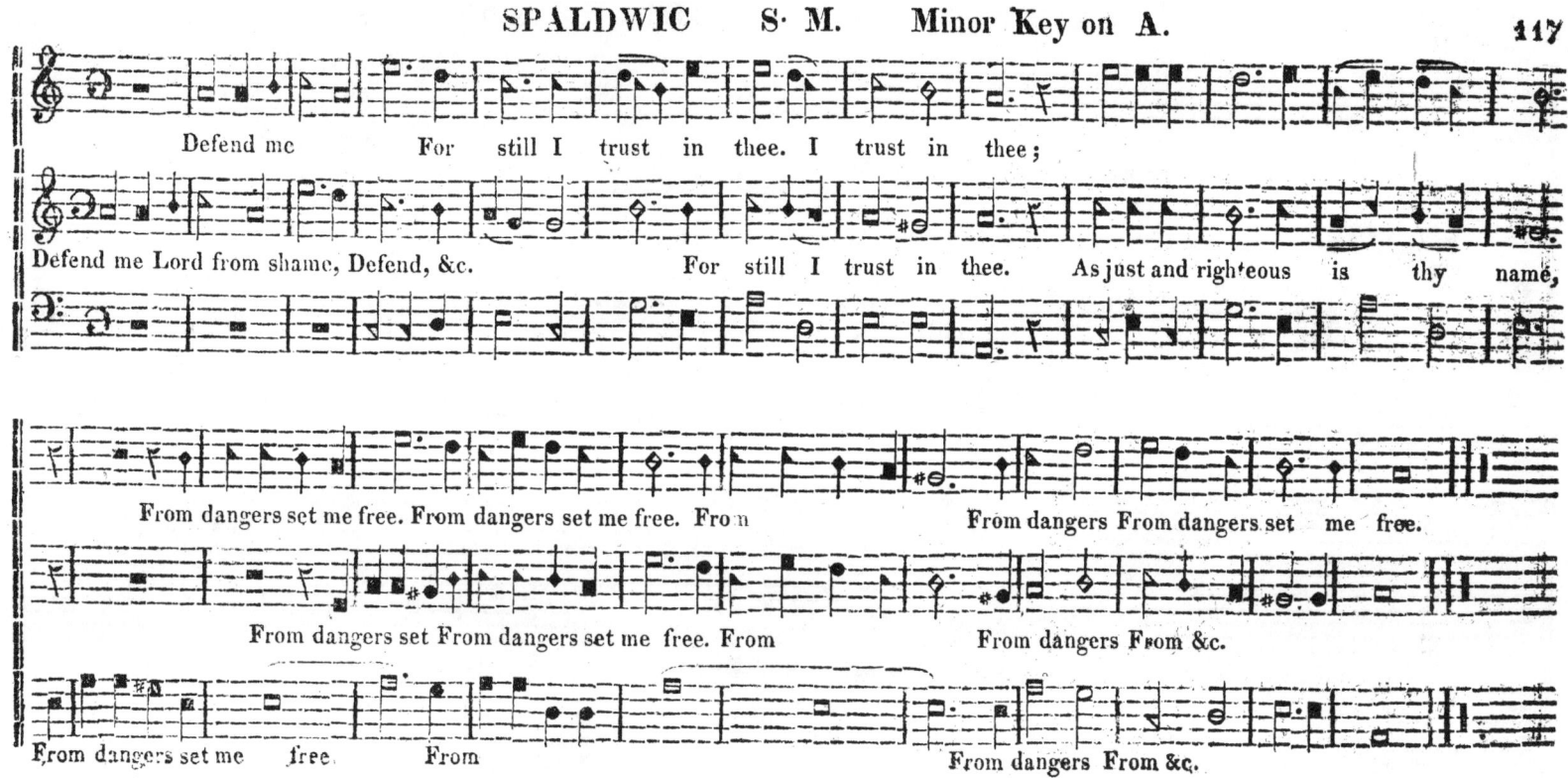

Defend me   For still I trust in thee. I trust in thee;

Defend me Lord from shame, Defend, &c.   For still I trust in thee.   As just and righteous is thy name,

From dangers set me free. From dangers set me free. From   From dangers From dangers set me free.

From dangers set From dangers set me free. From   From dangers From &c.

From dangers set me free. From   From dangers From &c.

118   SAPPHO.   11's & 5   Major Key on C.

When the fierce north wind, with his airy forces, Rears up the Baltic to a foaming fury, And the red lightning with a storm of hail, come's,

And the red lightning, with a storm of hail, comes, And the red lightning with a storm of hail, comes Rushing amain down.

HERMIT. 11. Minor Key on E.

Tis night, and the landscape is lovely no more; For morn is approaching your charms to restore,

I mourn, but ye woodlands I mourn not for you; Perfum'd with fresh fragrance & glitt'ring with dew:

Nor yet for the ravage of winter I mourn, But when shall spring visit the mouldering urn!

Kind nature the embryo blossoms shall save, O when shall it dawn on the night of the grave!

FRIENDSHIP 9's 8's & 6. Major Key on C.

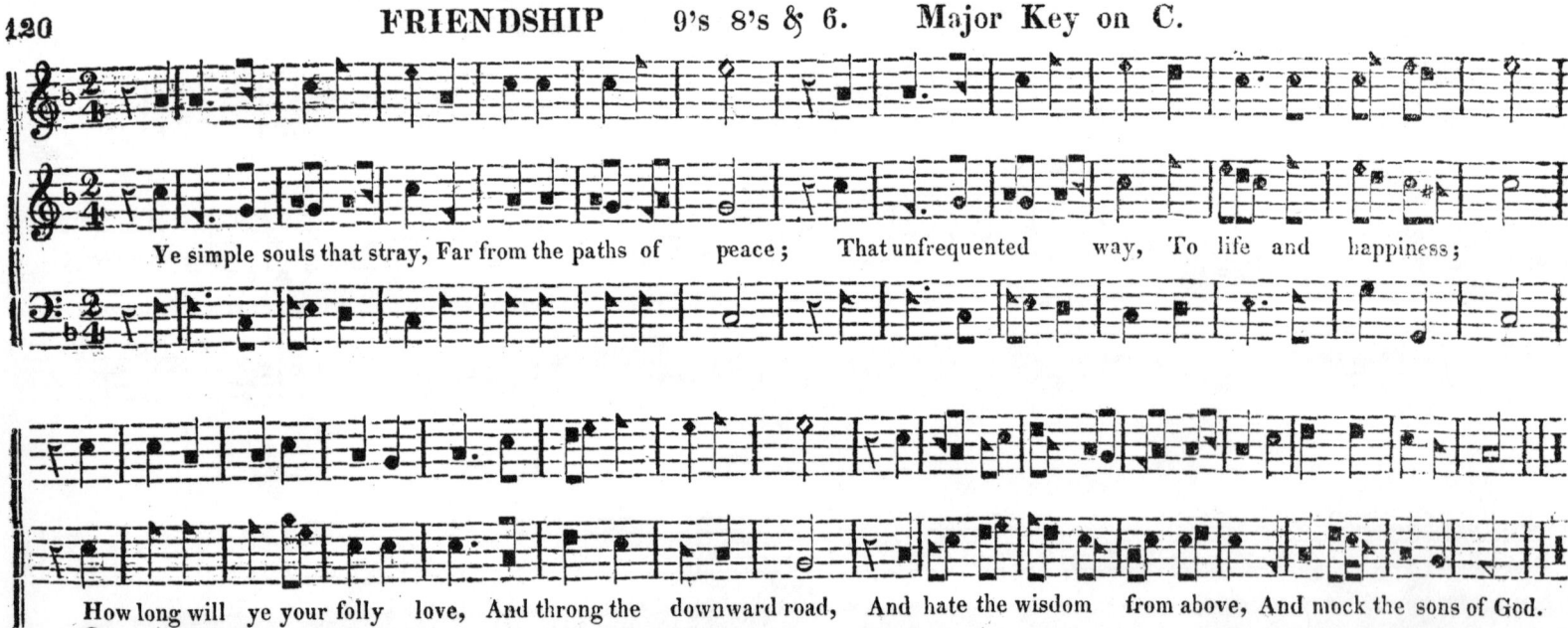

Ye simple souls that stray, Far from the paths of peace; That unfrequented way, To life and happiness;

How long will ye your folly love, And throng the downward road, And hate the wisdom from above, And mock the sons of God.

2 Madness and misery Ye count our life beneath, And nothing great can see, Or glorious in our death!
As born to suffer and to grieve, Beneath your feet we lie; and utterly contemn'd we live And unlamented die.

3 Poor, pensive sojourners, O'erwhelmed with grief and woes, Perplex'd with needless fears, And pleasures mortal foes;
More irksome than a gaping tomb, Our sight ye cannot bear, Wrapt in the melancholy gloom Of fanciful despair.

4 So wretched and obscure, The men whom ye despise, So foolish, weak and poor, above your scorn we rise.
Our conscience in the Holy Ghost, Can witness better things: For he whose blood is all our boast, Hath made us priests and Kings.

HEAVENLY UNION. 8's. Major Key on G.

Come, saints and sinners, hear me tell The wonders of Emmanuel, Who sav'd me from a burning hell, And brought my soul with him to dwell, And gave me heav'nly union.

2 When Christ the Saviour from on high, Beheld my soul in ruins lie; He look'd on me with pitying eye, And said to me as he pass'd by, "With God you have no union."
3 Then I began to weep and cry; I look'd this way and that to fly; It griev'd me sore that I must die; I strove salvation for to buy; But still I had no union.
4 But when I hated all my sin My dear Redeemer took me in; And with his blood he wash'd me clean; And O what seasons I have seen, E'er since I felt this union.
5 I prais'd the Lord both night and day; I went from house to house to pray; And if I met one on the way, I found I'd something still to say About this heavenly union.
6 I wonder not why saints do sing And praise the Lord upon the wing; And make the heavenly arches ring, With loud hosannahs to their king Who brought their souls to union.
7 O come backsliders come away, And mind to do, as well as say, And learn to watch as well as pray, And bear your cross from day to day; And then you'll feel this union.
8 We soon shall leave all things below, And quit these climes of pain below, And then we'll all to glory go, And there we'll see, and hear and know, And feel a perfect union.
9 Come heaven and earth unite your lays, And give to Jesus endless praise, And thou my soul look on and gaze! He bleeds, he dies, your debt he pays To give you heav'nly union.
10 O could I like an angel sound Salvation through the earth around; The devil's kingdom to confound; And triumph on Emmanuel's ground, And spread the heav'nly union.

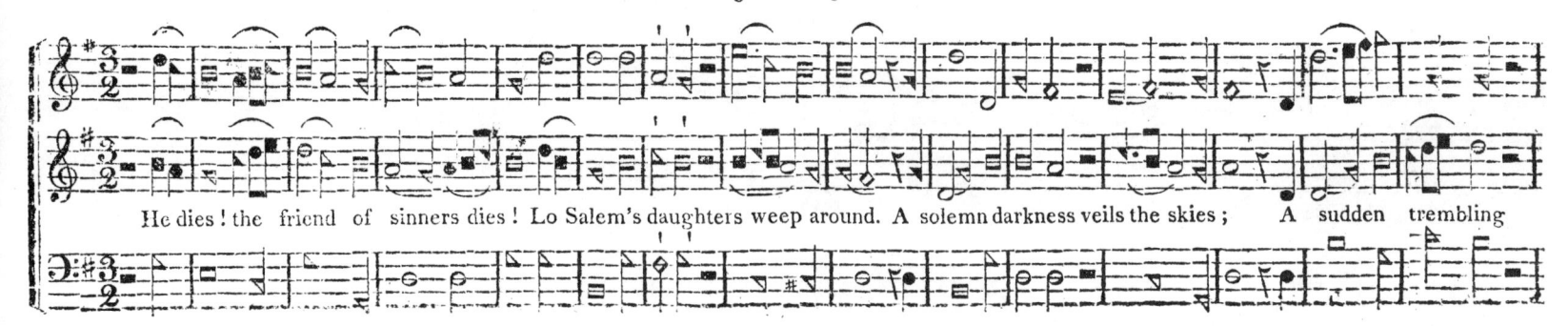

EASTER. Major Key on G.

He dies! the friend of sinners dies! Lo Salem's daughters weep around. A solemn darkness veils the skies; A sudden trembling

Easter, continued.

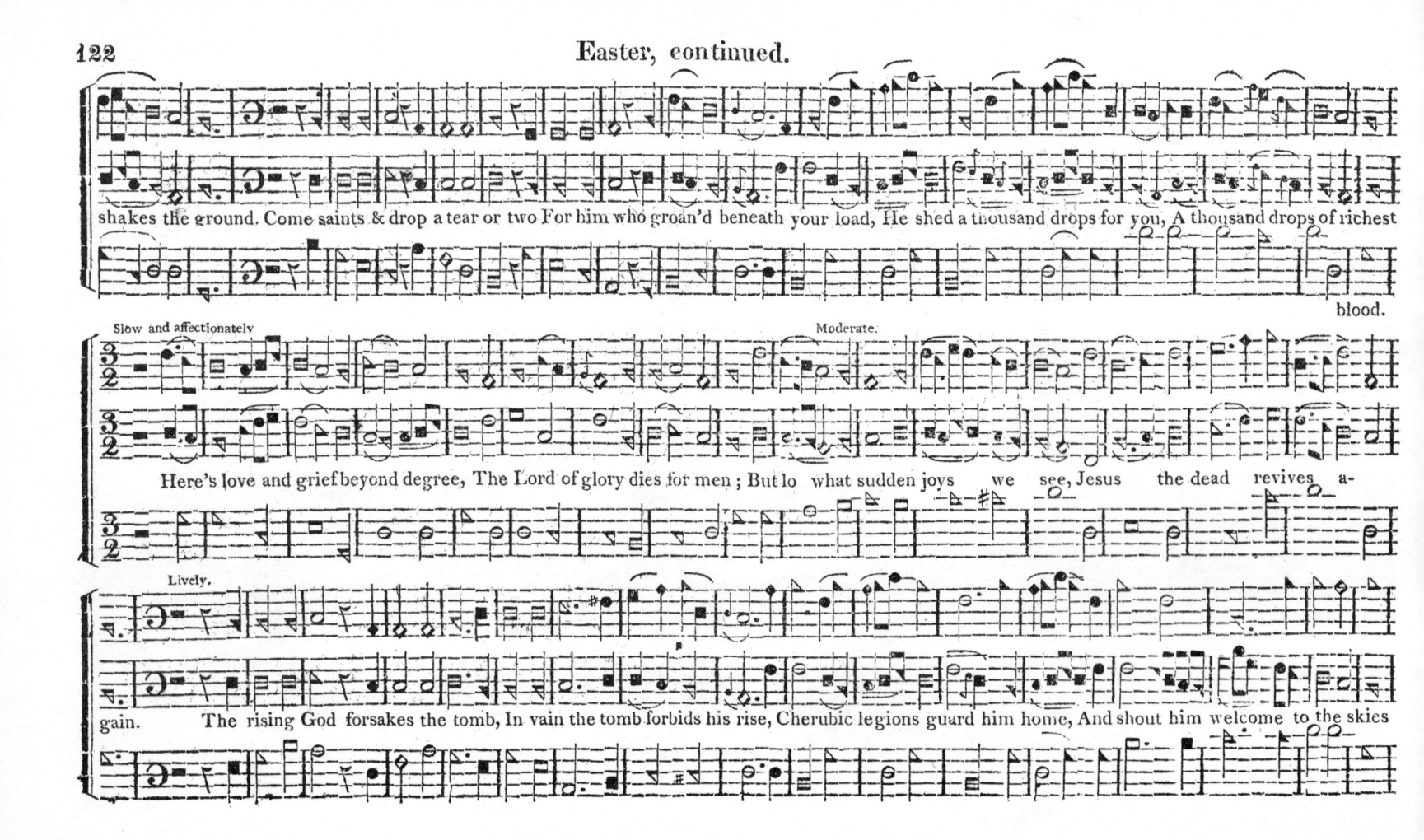

shakes the ground. Come saints & drop a tear or two For him who groan'd beneath your load, He shed a thousand drops for you, A thousand drops of richest blood.

Slow and affectionately. Moderate.

Here's love and grief beyond degree, The Lord of glory dies for men; But lo what sudden joys we see, Jesus the dead revives a-

Lively.

gain. The rising God forsakes the tomb, In vain the tomb forbids his rise, Cherubic legions guard him home, And shout him welcome to the skies

Easter, continued. 123

Soft. ... *Repeat loud.*

Break off your tears, ye saints, and tell How high your great Deliv'rer reigns. Sing how he spoil'd the hosts of hell, And led the monster death in chains.

Live for ever wond'rous King, Born to redeem and strong to save, Then ask the monster where's thy sting? And where's thy victory boasting grave? And where's thy victory boasting grave?

124   BETHLEHEM.   C. M.   Major Key on E.

While shepherds watch'd their flocks by night, All seated on the ground, The angel of the Lord came down, And glo- ry shone around / The angel of the Lord came down, And glory shone a- round The angel of the Lord came down, And glory shone a- rou- / The angel of the Lord came down, And glory shone a- round. The / The angel And glory shone, And glory shone a- rou-

Bethlehem, Continued.

125

Lord came down, And glory shone, And-nd, And glo- - -ry, And glo- - -ry, And glory shone a- round.

angel of the Lord came down, And

PARTICIPATION. C. M. Major Key on G.

Moderate.

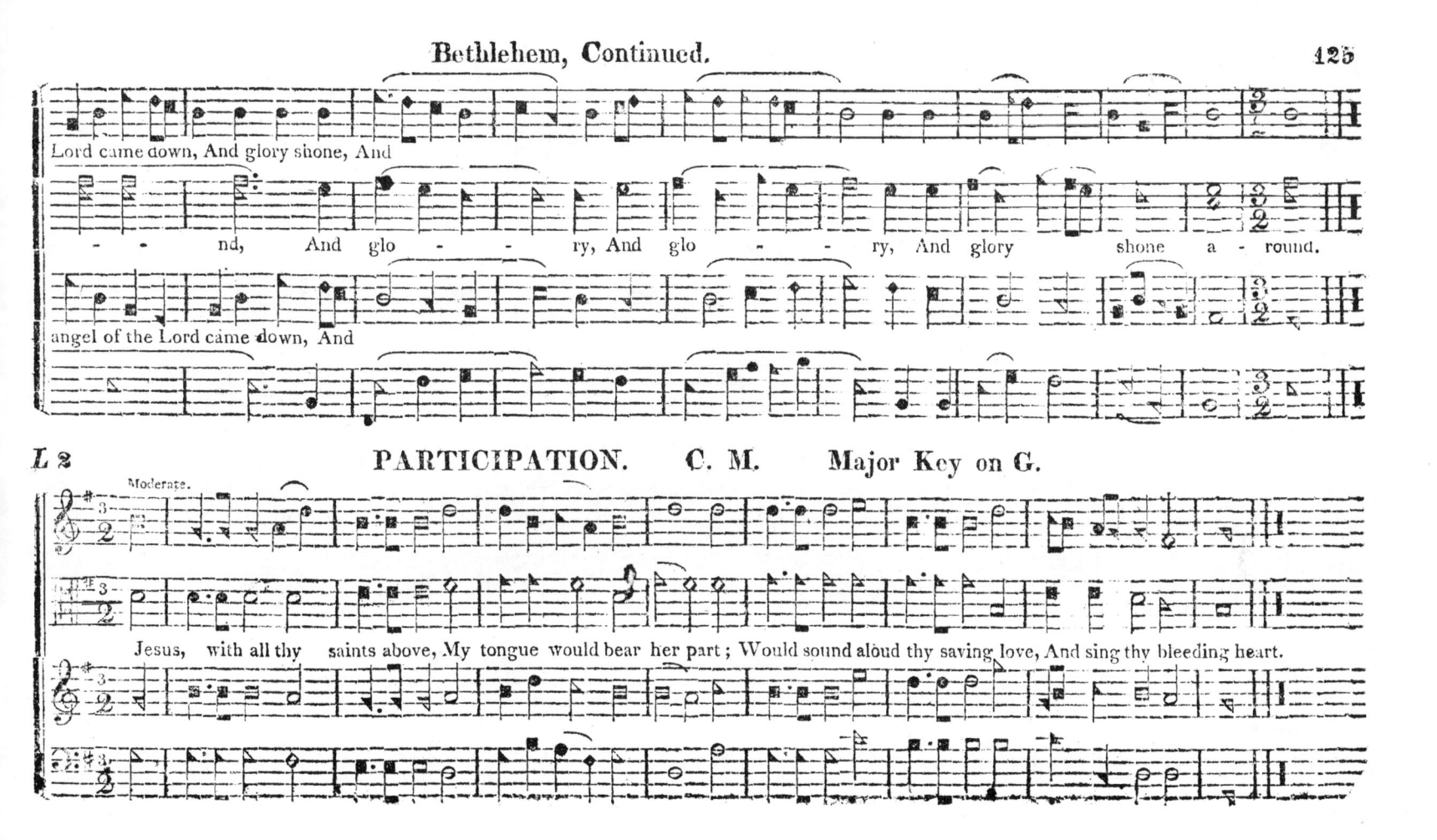

Jesus, with all thy saints above, My tongue would bear her part; Would sound aloud thy saving love, And sing thy bleeding heart.

126 HOLLIS. C. M. Minor Key on D.

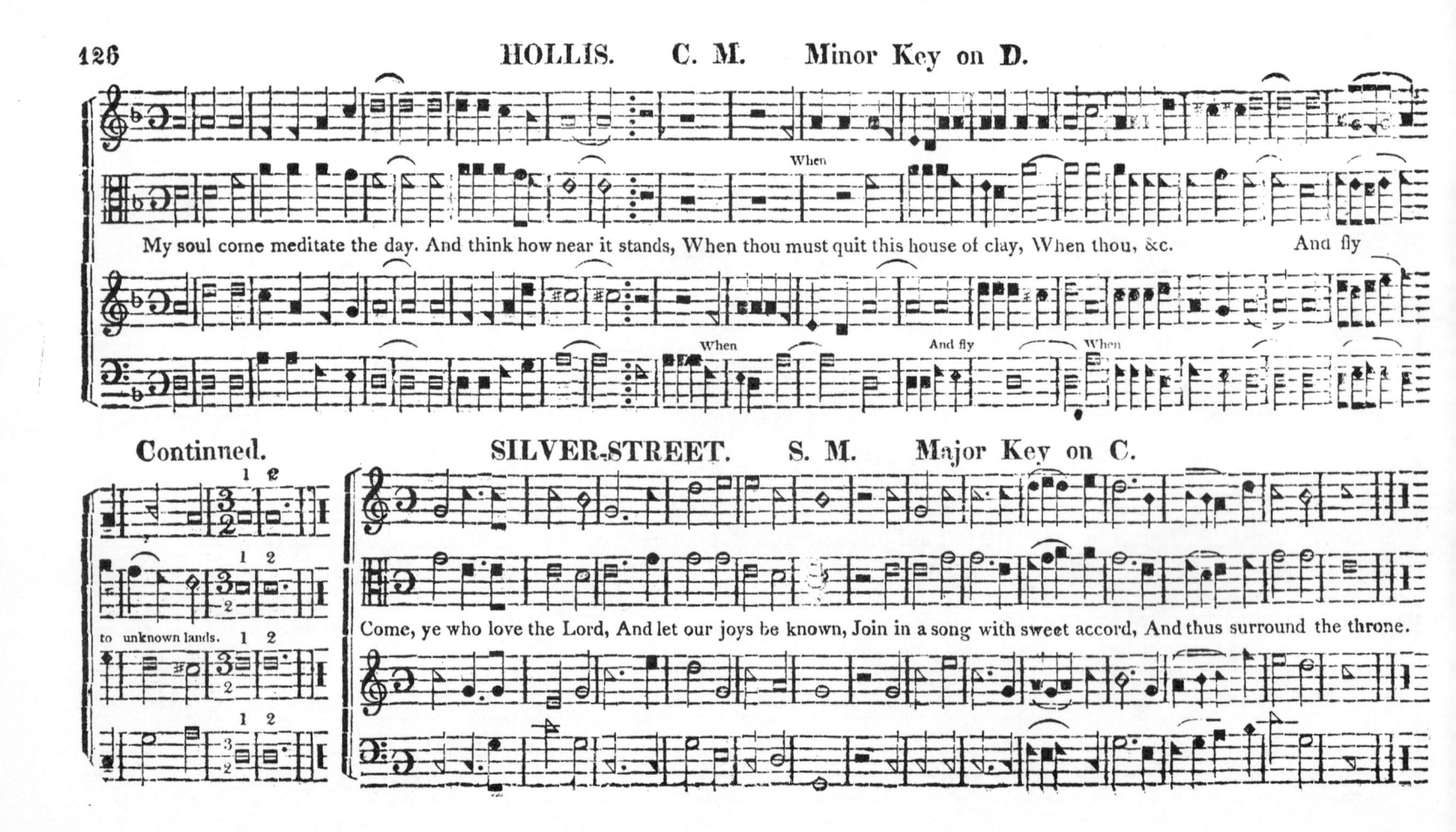

My soul come meditate the day. And think how near it stands, When thou must quit this house of clay, When thou, &c.   And fly

Continued. SILVER-STREET. S. M. Major Key on C.

to unknown lands.

Come, ye who love the Lord, And let our joys be known, Join in a song with sweet accord, And thus surround the throne.

REDEEMING LOVE. 7's. Major Key on C. 127

Now begin the heav'nly theme, Sing aloud in Jesus' name; Sing aloud in Jesus' name;

Ye, who his salvation prove, Triumph in redeeming love. Triumph in redeeming love.

2. Mourning souls dry up your tears, Banish all your guilty fears ; See your guilt and curse remove, Cancell'd by redeeming love.
3. Welcome all, by sin opprest, Welcome to his sacred rest ; Nothing brought him from above, Nothing but redeeming love.
4. Hither, then, your music bring, Strike aloud each cheerful string, Mortals join the host above, Join to praise redeeming love.

PLAINFIELD. C. M. Major Key on G.

Let him to whom we now belong, His sov'reign right assert, And take up ev'ry thankful song, And ev'ry loving heart. He justly claims us for his own, Who bo't us with a price! The christian lives to Christ alone, To Christ alone he dies. To Christ alone he dies.

COWPER. L M. Minor Key on G. 129

Forgive the song that falls so low Beneath the gratitude I owe; It means thy praise however poor, An angel's song can do no more, It means thy praise, however poor, An angel's song can do no more.

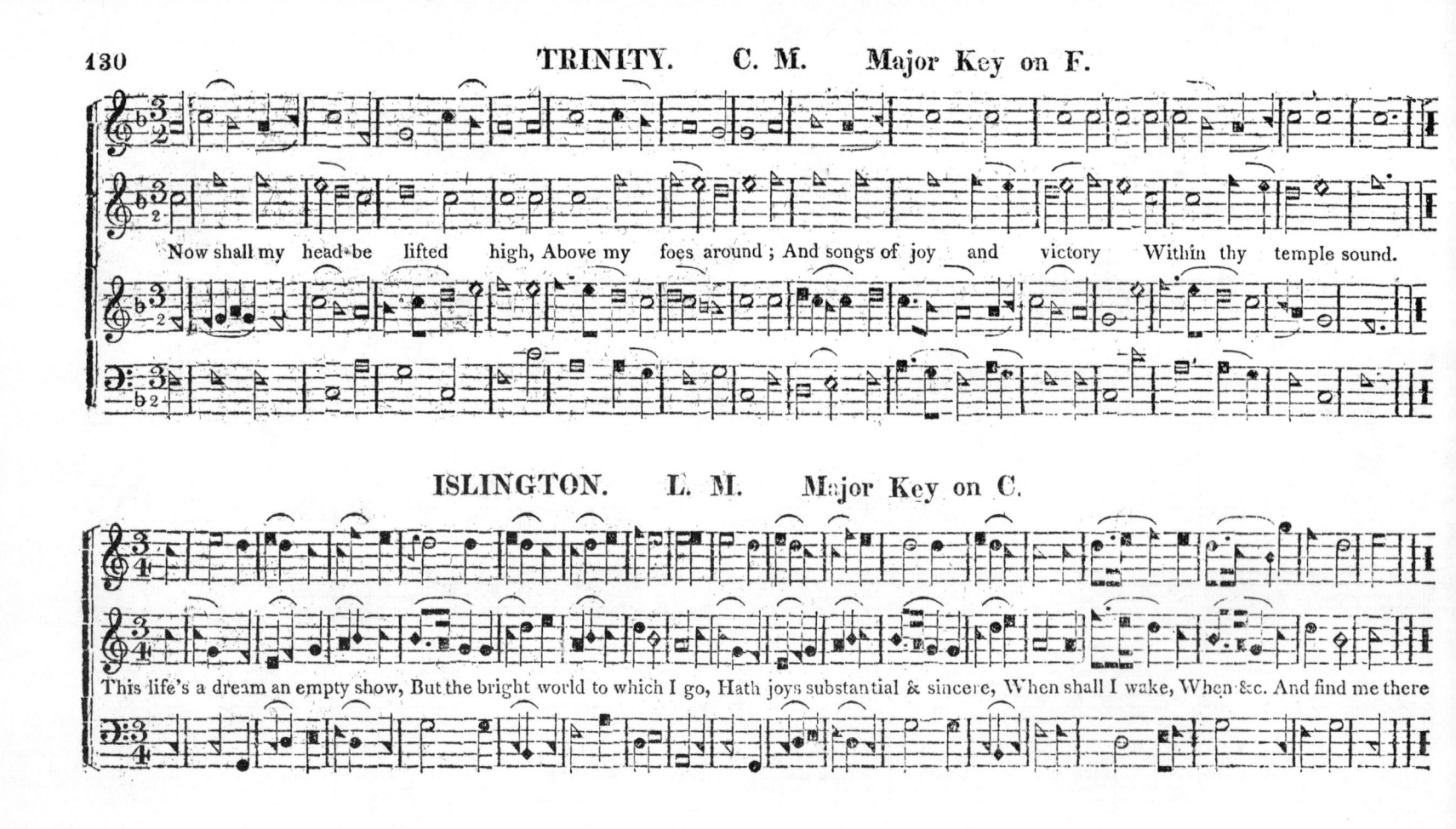

TRINITY. C. M. Major Key on F.

Now shall my head be lifted high, Above my foes around; And songs of joy and victory Within thy temple sound.

ISLINGTON. L. M. Major Key on C.

This life's a dream an empty show, But the bright world to which I go, Hath joys substantial & sincere, When shall I wake, When &c. And find me there

OMEGA. C. M. Major Key on C. 131

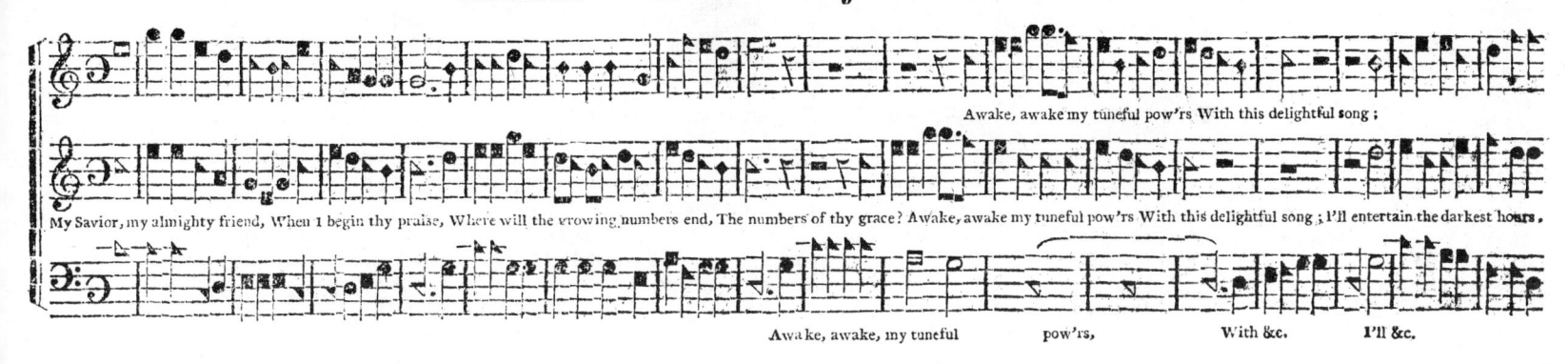

Awake, awake my tuneful pow'rs With this delightful song;

My Savior, my almighty friend, When I begin thy praise, Where will the growing numbers end, The numbers of thy grace? Awake, awake my tuneful pow'rs With this delightful song; I'll entertain the darkest hours.

Awake, awake, my tuneful pow'rs, With &c. I'll &c.

Continued.

Nor think the season long.

DOXOLOGY. Major Key on C.

Now unto the King eternal, immortal, invisible, the only wise God, Be honor, and glory, thro Jesus Christ, forever & ever, amen.

INDEX.

Names	Metre	Authors	Page
*Adoration	C		101
Africa	C	Billings	111
All Saints New	L	Hall	88
*Animation	8 & 7		108
*Babylonian Captivity	P	Dare	39
Band of Love			99
*Bellevue	P	Dare	38
Bethlehem	C	Billings	124
Boston	C	Billings	35
Boston	C		77
Brewer	L		18
*Bridgetown	S	Dare	43
Canaan	C		23
Castle Street	L	Madan	68
Christian Song	L		58
*Christmas Hymn	11's		79
Communion	C	Robison	103
*Concert	8 & 7		113
*Consolation	C		20
*Consolation	8's 6 & 8's		105
Content	S		69
Cowper	L	Holding	129
David's Lamentation		Billings	115
*Davis	11 & 8		81
Dawning Light	10's		28
*Dependence	S	Findlay	78
*Dismission	P	Dare	47
Doxology		Selby	131
Easter		Madan	121
Egypt	S	Madan	23
Exhortation	L	Doolittle	55
Exhortation	C	Hibbert	90
*Fajuton	C	Dare	42
*Fall of Babylon			44
Farewell Anthem		French	84
*Fidelia	C	Lewer	56
*Fiducia	C	Robison	20
*Forster	C		40
Friendship	6 8 6		120
Friendship	8 6 8 6 8 8 6		102
Gallilee	L	Madan	111
Ganges	8 8 6		98
Georgia	C		30
German Hymn	L	Pleyel	114
*Glasgow	L	Dare	42
Gospel Trumpet	8's & 4		27
*Gospel Trump		Dare	37
*Hallelujah	8 & 7		112
Hamilton	L	Madan	32
Happiness	6's		98
Harmony	10's & 11's		30
*Heavenly Union	8's		121
Hermit	11's		119
Hinsdale	C	Holyoke	90
Hollis	C	Holden	126
Hundred and Forty-eighth	L		70
Interrogation	S		76
Invitation	L	Kimball	96
Isle of White	C		25
Islington	L		130
Judgment Anthem		Morgan	60
*Kedron	L	Dare	43
Kingwood	7's	Peck	92
Lamentation	L		83
*Landaff	S	Findlay	71
*Liberty	C		59
Lonsdale	S		116
Madison	L	Read	51
*Marcus Hook	C	Dare	89
Mendom		Billings	106
Meiton	6's & 9	Madan	26
Messiah	8's 6 8's & 6		109
*Middle Paxton	P	Austin	57
Miles Lane	C	Shrubsole	93
*Millville	L	Dare	39
*Minister's Farewell	C		112
Missionary	C		50
*Morality			103
Mountain	C		82
*Mount Hope		Dare	46
Mount Pleasant	C	Madan	24
Mount Zion	S	Brown	22
Nativity			31
*New Canaan	C		101
Newmark	C	Bull	77
*New Monmouth	8 7 8 7		104
*Ninety-Fifth	C	Chapin	21
*Ninety-Third	S	Chapin	24
Northfield	C	Ingalls	92
Old German	5's 6 & 5		47
Omega	C	Holden	131
Pardoning Grace	L		93
Participation	C	Arne	125
Pastoral	L P	Madan	110
*Perseverance	11's		104
Phœbus	C	Billings	36
Pilgrim's Farewell			41
Plainfield	C	Kimball	128
*Power	L	White	100
Plymouth Dock	L		29
*Redeeming Grace	9 & 8		79
Redeeming Love	7's	Madan	127
*Redemption Anthem			48
Restoration	10 & 11		104
*Roadstown	P	Dare	45
*Rockbridge	L	Chapin	95
*Rockingham	C	Chapin	97
Saint Johns	8 8 6		33
Saint John's	L	Billings	100
Saint Michael's	P	Handel	95
Salford	C	Madan	113
Sappho	11's & 5	Billings	118
Schenectady	L	Shumway	34
Seaman's Song	L		114
Sharon	S		18
Shields	s & 7		29
Shields	C		102
Silver Street	S	Smith	126
*Solicitude	11 & 8		109
*Solitude	S	M'Kyes	76
Sounding Joy	C		78
Spaldwick	S		117
*Spring Hill	P		94
*Sterling	S		107
*Sublimity			101
Thanksgiving Anthem		Selby	72
*Transport	12 & 11		106
Thrinty	C	Tansur	130
*Triumph	11's		80
Trumpet	L		25
Twenty-Third	L	Bull	81
*Twenty-Fourth	C	Chapin	20
Twenty-Fifth	S	Gillet	28
*Unitia	10 11 10 11	Chapin	87
Vergennes	C		87
Vermont		Billings	19
Vernon	L	Chapin	21
Vienna		Fremmer	105
Walsal	C	Tansur	69
Warren	L	Lane	68
Washington	L		108
Waterford	6's & 8		27
Williamstown	L	Brown	31
*Willington			100
*Wilmington	C	Dare	52
Winchester	7's		32
Windsor		Kirby	26
Woburn	L	Kimball	57
Worcester	L	Wood	91

Tunes marked thus * are new.